OUR CHALLENGE

Rabbi Meir Kahane
OUR CHALLENGE
The Chosen Land

CHILTON BOOK COMPANY, *Radnor, Pennsylvania*

Copyright © 1974 by Meir Kahane
First Edition   All Rights Reserved
Published in Radnor, Pa., by Chilton Book Company
and simultaneously in Ontario, Canada
by Thomas Nelson & Sons, Ltd.
Designed by Adrianne Onderdonk Dudden
Manufactured in the United States of America

LIBRARY OF CONGRESS CATALOGING IN PUBLICATION DATA

Kahane, Meir.
  Our challenge; the chosen land.
  1. Religious Zionism. 2. Israel. 3. Jewish-Arab relations. I. Title.
DS150.R32K33 1974   956.94'001   74-661
ISBN 0-8019-6023-1

*Dedicated to the memory of
Baruch Cohen, hero of the nation*

*May the L-rd avenge his blood that was spilled
in Madrid, Shvat, 5733*

Contents

1	*The Challenge*	**13**
2	*The Chosen Land*	**20**
3	*The Chosen People: Questions*	**54**
4	*The Chosen People: Definitions*	**90**
5	*The Chosen State: The Jew Without*	**112**
6	*The Chosen State: The Jew Within*	**140**
7	*The Chosen State: Character and Personality*	**156**
8	*The Destiny*	**172**

For thou art a holy people unto the L-rd thy G-d: the L-rd thy G-d hath chosen thee to be a special people unto himself, above all people that are upon the face of the earth.
—Deuteronomy 7:6

Every place whereon the soles of your feet shall tread shall be yours: from the wilderness and Lebanon, from the river, the river Euphrates, even unto the uttermost sea shall your coast be.
There shall be no man be able to stand before you: for the L-rd your G-d shall lay the fear of you and the dread of you upon all the land that ye shall tread upon, as he hath said unto you.
—Deuteronomy 11:24-25

OUR CHALLENGE

1
The Challenge

There *is* a Jewish destiny. That which happened to the Jewish people in the past, that which occurs in our times, that which will happen in the days and years to come, is not haphazard, a game of chance. The Jewish people plays its role in history within the limits of divine ordinance.

We stand today, all of us—leaders, captains, elders, men, women, and little ones—before a great moment in history. Those of us who have been chosen, for some inexplicable reason, to live in these times of unparalleled disasters and unequaled miracles of triumph must surely sense in every fiber of our being that the things that we have seen and experienced are not mere chance.

The soul-shattering Holocaust that ripped away a third of our people, followed immediately by the incredible ending of the incredible Exile, the creation of the third Jewish commonwealth, the Ingathering of the Exiles from the four corners of the earth, the smashing of the enemy in Six Days and the return to the Wall and the liberated lands of Judea and Samaria—all are parts of the great moment in history before which we stand.

It is clear that the Almighty is prepared to bring us into the final deliverance and that the beginning of the redemption is under way. We stand at a historic moment of deliverance.

But great moments must be seized. They wait to be grasped. They always join together the ultimate deliverance with a potential for preceding disaster. Salvation is invariably coupled with a possible attendant tragedy that wipes away the human blemish with the terrible scourge of pain and suffering.

It need not be. The great moments that proclaim oncoming deliverance wait for an instant to be understood and grasped. If we recognize them and respond to them, we are blessed. If we do not, they disappear from view and make us pay a tragic and terrible price before the advent of the deliverance.

And the most terrible part of the price is its *avoidability:* the fact that it need not have been paid had we understood and acted.

The great tasks of our day are to clearly and boldly define, teach, and implement.

To define clearly and precisely the purpose and destiny of the Jewish people; the purpose and reason for the Land of Israel and the state therein; the relationship between the Jew and the state; the relationship between the Jew of the state and the Jew in the Exile; the total aim and destiny of the Jew, his people, land, and state.

To teach and implement that definition boldly and relentlessly; to create the kind of Jew and the kind of Jewish people that is their sole reason for being; to create the uniquely Jewish kind of state and policy within the Land of Israel that is the sole reason for having one; to create the kind of relationship between Jew and Jew and Jew and state that is the only true and honest one in terms of Jewishness.

In a word, our people must be a Jewish people, not a pale replica of others. Our state must not seek merely to be like all the rest, but a distinctively Jewish one.

The Jewish people stands or falls on the knowledge that it is *not* like all other people. The foundation of foundations and the raison d'être of the Jewish people is that it is the Chosen People, a godly people—the people chosen by the Almighty to do his will. It is a people that was called into being by G-d and whose existence and fate are decreed by him. And from this chosenness, this call to holiness and challenge to greatness, flow certain absolute and necessary axioms. If we are chosen, then we are a certain kind of people with a certain kind of role and a certain kind of state. There is a Chosen People, a chosen land, a chosen state, and a chosen destiny, and the conduct of the Jew and his state must be directed toward that destiny. The normal rules of nationhood and statehood do not apply to us; the normal logic of foreign policy is not ours. If we obey the call of the Jewish destiny and the command of the Almighty we shall endure and live, both in this world and the next. If we do not return to the Jewish role, we will pay a terrible price before the ultimate redemption comes, wiping away our sins with the suffering of pain and war.

The creation of the Jewish people and its survival has a divine purpose. The rebirth of the State of Israel and the miracles that have accompanied that rebirth are part of that purpose. It has been ordained that the Jewish people return home and rebuild their Jewish lives in their land—all of it. Are we capable of understanding this and the fact that only a truly *Jewish* state is the aim of the divine decree? If we do, we will hasten the advent of the redemption; if we do not, we will not only lengthen it but we will pay a terrible price in the form of our own sufferings and the soul-sufferings of our youth.

Today our youth, many of them, stand confused. Tomorrow there will be more of them and the ideas that to their elders seem basic and easy to understand will not be obvious or clearly understood. We have taken these ideas as well as our youth for granted, and we stand to lose them both. That will be the price of our neglect and mistaken self-assurance. We have not given our youth the most basic of human needs, the idea—the *Jewish* idea. Our youth wait for it, as a hungry man for bread. They wait and are prepared to accept—if we give it.

The idea is the weapon. If you have it and believe in it, if you teach it and spread it, if you organize pupils who will teach it and spread it to others, you can change a world. For actions and reactions are predicated upon ideas, and depending on the idea we will act and react in a certain way—correctly or wrongly, with truth or with falsehood.

We in the State of Israel are in a struggle for the souls of the generation that is growing into manhood. If we wish to win them—and not lose them either to the enemy or to the well-meaning fools who would destroy us just as effectively—we must have the *idea,* believe in it completely and teach it unceasingly. We must fill the minds and hearts and souls of our youth with it daily.

Let us not make the most dangerous of all errors, and believe that ideological vacuums can remain. Just like their physical counterparts, they must and will be filled by something or someone. And there are people and groups today who are working hard and tirelessly to fill the fertile minds of our youth with their own ideology. Let us not underestimate them or their numbers. Let us not be so foolish as to believe that small numbers mean impotency or that sacred cows remain permanently sacred.

That which seems indubitably true and axiomatic to us is not necessarily so for the next generation. What is holy to one leaves the second indifferent, while the third looks upon it as profane. We *can* lose our youth and we can watch them lose *our* values through our apathy and indifference, our failure to give them burning ideals to match the ideas of others. We can also lose them through weak, unconvincing arguments that leave the youth troubled, dissatisfied, and unfulfilled. And if we lose the battle for our youth, we will ultimately lose *every* other battle.

The battle has already started. Already the Left, the wreckers and the moral anarchists, have made deep ideological gains among the youth even though we, in our preoccupation with the more prosaic things in life, do not recognize it. The Left has always understood the power of ideas. It is time that the nationalist camp understood this also. The primary battleground is not the Knesset but the schools, the campuses, the streets—wherever our youth and their minds are.

As one who spends much time among every section of our youth, I can see the danger *and the potential opportunity*. In these pages I shall try to present ideas, Jewish ideas that your youth will accept and cherish.

Although these ideas are my own, clearly they represent much of the thinking of the Jewish Defense League in Israel. It would be logical to assume that the program of the League in the Jewish state will be based upon many of the ideas in this book. Just as there is a need for *physical* defense, we believe, so is there at least as great a need for *spiritual* defense.

The ideas put forward in this book are not only sound ideas; more important, they are *Jewish* ideas, drawn from Jewish sources and tradition. In the end, that is the only honest program for a Jewish state and a Jewish individual. That which marks us as different and which gives us a right and reason to set ourselves up as a separate nationality, state, and entity is our unique Jewishness. That Jewishness can only be expressed through Jewish concepts and those concepts can only be derived from Jewish sources. In short, I intend simply to restore the fundamental thoughts of Judaism. The pity is that many Jews have never stopped to listen to them.

There may, therefore, be many who will be upset by some of the ideas in this book. Yet they cannot claim that these are not Jewish ideas that have throughout the centuries represented the mainstream of Jewish thought. Those who oppose them would do well to honestly search their own minds and hearts and to discover whether *their* ideas are not really the products of intellectual and ideological assimilation.

I love the Jewish people and think that there is no greater and deeper pride than that of knowing that one is a Jew. I love the Jewish state, the Land of Israel, and see in it the hand of the Almighty, the realization of the vision of the Prophets. And precisely because one loves the Jew and the land, must he speak up in admonition and criticism. So long as one is motivated by love, that admonition and demand for change are not only valid but obligatory. I would do the same for my sons and daughters, precisely because I love them so. If I did not I would not care what they did or what they would become. It is because a Jew must love his people and state, must care about them and their fate, that it is so important that we define the Jewish people and state, and work to create them in the image of Jewishness.

2
The Chosen Land

In the year 135 the Judean fortress of Bethar fell to the Roman legions of the Emperior Hadrian. In a bloody confrontation tens of thousands fell. The leader of the Judean revolt, the legendary "son of a star," Bar Kochba, was found dead, and the people of Judea were scattered to the four corners of the earth, there to begin an Exile unprecedented in persecution, in stubborn survival, and in faith in Return.

Hadrian, furious with the stubborn and rebellious

people, undertook to totally eradicate their pernicious faith and to wipe out the memory of their nationhood and land. Edicts were issued—accompanied by the death penalty in case of violation—forbidding the Jewish Sabbath to be observed, outlawing the circumcision of children, and banning the study of Torah. Under the supervision of the procurator Rufus, the plow was drawn over the city of Jerusalem and the Temple Mount as a sign that Zion was forever buried, and plans for a new city, Roman in form and pagan in character, were drawn up. The name Jerusalem was erased and the new city called Aelia Capitolina. A column was erected in honor of Hadrian, and memorials, temples, and statues dedicated to Roman, Greek, and Phoenician gods defiled the Holy Land.

One other thing was done. The name of Judea, the home of the Jewish people, was changed to Palestine. Had Hadrian suppressed his desire to erase the memory of Jews and their state, and not changed its name, it is conceivable that the Jews of Israel would be faced today with "Judean" terrorists.

The time has come to declare a policy for Israel and its Jewish supporters that clearly, loudly, and pointedly proclaims that there never was, there is not now, and there never will be such a thing as a "Palestine" people or state. The Land of Israel, Eretz Yisroel, is the land of the Jewish people, and no one else's, in all its historical boundaries. In the face of public and strident Arab hate and threats to destroy us totally, all those who live under the illusion that "compromise" will bring peace and security to Israel are either fools or knaves.

The only hope for the Jewish people to preserve their own state and existence, a right claimed by all peoples, is to hold on to every inch of the land they liberated in 1967, push with all their strength for a massive Jewish immigration and settlement in all parts of the land, and promote a program that will convince the hostile Arab minority both in the liberated lands and in the "little Israel" of pre-June 1967 that their own best interests would be served by emigrating to other lands. Let us examine these points more carefully.

On a clear night more than three millennia ago, a man named Abraham stood in the desert and heard the voice of G-d say: ". . . . Lift up now thine eyes and look from the place where thou art, northward and southward and eastward and westward, for all the land which thou seest, to thee will I give it and to thy seed forever. And I will make thy seed as the dust of the earth, so that if a man can number the dust of the earth then shall thy seed also be numbered. Arise, walk through the land in the length of it and in the breadth of it; for I will give it unto thee (Genesis 13: 14-17). The promise of the L-rd to the first Jew was repeated to his son and to his: "Sojourn in this land . . . unto Abraham thy father" (Genesis 26: 3-4); "And, behold . . . . of the earth be blessed" (Genesis 28: 13-14). And the promised boundaries of the Land were clearly stated to the father of the nation: "In that same day . . . . and the Jebusites" (Genesis 15: 18-21).

"Unto the L-rd is the earth and all that is in it." The creator of the universe, who gives and takes away, gave unto his people the Land of Israel as theirs, alone and without reservation. This is the Jewish claim to

The Chosen Land 23

Israel. Upon this claim the children of Israel returned from the slavery of Egypt to liberate the land and create their Kingdom. Upon this claim they lived there for hundreds of years from the time of Joshua until the destruction of the first Temple. Upon this claim they returned from their Babylonian exile to set up yet another Jewish state that survived hundreds of years more. *On this claim they wandered through two millennia of exile, never forgetting, daily repeating their claim to the land from which they were driven, surviving until political Zionism realized the vision that the believing Jew had kept alive.*

There is a Jewish people, the same that began with Abraham. There is a Jewish state, the home of that Jewish people from the time of the first divine promise. This is the Jewish claim. It is not a request. It is not an offer. It is not a plea. It is a claim and it brooks no denial. We have no home but Israel; we have no claim to any home but Israel. But within this one small state, that claim is absolute. The Land of Israel is the land of the Jewish people, whose claim to sovereignty over it—*all of it*—is clear and as ancient as G-d's decision to grant that sovereignty.

A "Palestine" people? The concept is a contradiction in terms. There is either a "Palestine" or a Land of Israel, and we declare for the latter. There is no "Palestine" and if there is no "Palestine," there is no "Palestine" people. Arabs? Yes. Those Arabs who dwell and who dwelt for years within Eretz Yisroel are indeed part of the Arab people or nation and we respect and recognize that definition. But they are not "Palestinians," for there never was such a concept. The Arabs who wandered into the Land of Israel while it lay desolate and empty of its exiled Jewish sons and daughters came as trespassers and interlopers. The passage of time, no matter how much time, cannot make legal that which is illegal. The claim of Arabs to have lived within the land for years or centuries is irrelevant in terms of a claim to Arab national sovereignty. And how much more so when "Palestine" was always looked upon as nothing more than southern Syria. As individuals who arrived and lived in the Land of Israel while there was no Jewish state, they are free to live and prosper. Under claim of national right, they are entitled to nothing. Jews have a sovereign national right to the land as a people and under this, each Jew has a *right* to live in Israel. The Arab, with no national sovereignty claim, may ask to be allowed to live in Eretz Yisroel, but can expect nothing more than that.

It is this most basic of concepts that gives Jews not only the right to their own state, but the right to a state within the entire boundaries of the Land of Israel. Neither a fictitious "Palestine" nor a no less fictitious "Jordan" are anything more than interlopers within the boundaries of Eretz Yisroel. To be sure, the Jewish leaders in 1947 reluctantly accepted a Jewish state whose boundaries were not only absurdities but enclosed only a small fraction of Eretz Yisroel. Their acceptance of these boundaries in no way meant acquiescence in any foreign claim to parts of Eretz Yisroel but a willingness to accept a desperately needed state and a condition of peace. Their motives were not acquiescence in or recognition of foreign claims, or the waiving of Jewish rights, but a desire for peace and a

The Chosen Land 25

postponing of Jewish claims until the Messiah comes and resolves *kushyot v'bayaot* (probelms and difficulties).

In return for peach and a genuine recognition of the Jewish richt to a state, Jews were willing, not to give up their rights, but not to press their rightful claims. But when the Arabs chose to deny *any* Jewish right and went to war, the Jewish claim to all the land that fell to its armies became clear. What happened in 1948 and again in 1967 was that Jewish land returned to its people. We do not seek war: one Jewish life is not worth all the Jewish land that is under foreign rule. But when war is forced upon us and Jewish bodies fall, then the historic land that returns to us remains—never to be returned.

What happened in the past can happen again in the future. The choice is that of our enemies. If they seek to retain that part of the Land of Israel which they hold, they need only make peace and, while we will not ever give up our claim, we will not press it. If they seek to persist in creating a "Palestine," they can do so on that part of Eretz Yisroel which is in their hands. We will not recognize their right to the name or the state but we will not press our claim. But should they again insist upon war, then much more Jewish territory will return to its rightful owners.

What is the Arab of Eretz Yisroel? A human being, and we respect him for that and must treat him accordingly. What else is he? A member of the Arab nation, and we respect him for that. But he is no more than that: he is not a "Palestinian" belonging to a "Palestine" state, because both designations are fictitious. The Jewish claim rests upon divine grant and historical continuity based on that grant, and even if there were no questions of security, the state and the boundaries of that state would be Jewish for historical reasons alone.

Yet there *is* a security question, a question that goes to the heart of the existence of the Jewish state and the lives of its inhabitants. This question of security concerns the liberated lands, the Arabs who live there, the Arabs of pre-1967 Israel and, indeed, the entire Arab-Israel conflict. All of these problems, from a security standpoint, have given rise to a number of dangerous illusions that we must look at carefully and dispel. We fail to do so at our own peril.

The first illusion can be stated as: "If only Israel shows 'moderation,' a willingness to 'compromise,' and is prepared to make 'concessions' to the Arabs, peace can be achieved."

Anyone who thinks this way encourages the destruction of Israel. Despite pious hopes and impious pressures, the fact remains that there will be no peace between Jews and Arabs so long as there remains a Jewish state of *any* kind, no matter how small. Regardless of what concessions Israel might make to the Arabs— be they the modest concessions of a Golda Meir or the maximalist concessions of the Israeli Left—*all* of the land that is now Israel is considered by the Arabs to be part of "Palestine." There is no difference to the "Palestinian" between the soil of Hebron on the West Bank or that over which are built the Jewish coastal villas of Herzliya and Savyon. "Shehem (Nablus) is like unto Tel Aviv and Haifa and Jericho are both mine," sayeth the Arab nationalist. So long as there remains a Jewish state with the name of Israel, the Arabs will never agree to peace.

If that is a depressing prognosis, far better for pundits to be depressed than for Israelis to succumb to false hopes and be exterminated.

One finds it difficult to understand those who claim that a return of the lands liberated in 1967 will bring peace closer. If that is the major drawback to peace in the Middle East, what in the world did Nasser want in 1967, when the Arabs *had* all the territory they now ask to be returned? On June 4, 1967, as the Arab world was consuming itself in an orgy of hate and describing in intimate detail what it was going to do when it captured Tel Aviv, all the areas it now wants returned as the price of "peace"—the Sinai, the Gaza Strip, the West Bank of the Jordan, the Golan Heights—were in its hands. What was the fight about then? And what was the fight about in 1956 when Nasser, with Soviet aid, prepared to wipe out an Israel that was *not* sitting in Hebron and Sinai as it does today? And what in heaven's name did the Arabs want returned in 1948 when the United Nations Partition Plan created a grotesque and impossible Jewish state that encompassed a mere 13 percent of the land* originally mandated by the League of Nations? In all the wars that the Arabs forced upon the Jews since 1948, and indeed in all the terror and pogroms of the Arab nationalists since 1919, the aim was clear: no Jewish State *at all*. This proposition, I put it, is unacceptable for the Jews of Israel. Thus, without a change of Arab heart, which is nowhere to be seen, there will be no peace.

---

*Including Transjordan.—Ed.

One laughs—but is not amused—at those who point to the statements made by certain Arabs that they are now willing to accept Israel's existence. In the face of the volumes of hate, threats, and solemn oaths to wipe out Israel, what conceivable faith can be placed in such obviously politically motivated statements? Having failed to wipe out Israel militarily and perceiving the need for world support, the Arabs must carefully, although temporarily, shelve the old truths and present a more modest and balanced image. "Throw the Jews into the sea? Heaven forbid! All we seek is a return of what is ours." It is an unfunny joke. The clear fact remains that even if an Arab leader exists who would seriously accept the existence of Israel, he would not long survive the signing of a pact and the pact would not long survive him.

Any pullback by Israel to the impossibly dangerous border of June 1967 would be followed by a denunciation of the peace agreement by Arab opposition elements and Israel would be faced with a fait accompli accompanied by at least three days of world sympathy.

Concessions? Compromise? Moderation? Foolish exercises in self-delusion and self-destruction so long as the Arab believes—as he does—that Israel is a bandit state and that the Jews have stolen "Palestine."

It is because we—more than the Jewish leftists and liberals—understand and respect the reality of Arab nationalism, that we realize the futility of expecting the nationalist to give up his dream. Would *we* give up our dream? Would *we* lose our hope? Neither will the Arab nationalist.

The problem is that time is always on the side of the tenacious; conversely, it is the enemy of the weary. The never-ending struggle erodes the determination to achieve total victory and pushes tired men into the search for solutions and compromises that are often more the product of the desire to rest than that of common sense.

Those who are tired allow themselves to believe what freshness of vigor would label as nonsense. Exhaustion and monotony push us into self-delusion. We become partners to our own destruction as we fool ourselves into believing that madness is sanity, war is peace, evil is good—all so that we might return to a life of peace and normalcy.

Time is also on the side of the aggressor and works against his intended victim. For it gradually washes out of our minds the past moment of danger, the time when the aggressor sought to attack, plunder, and destroy. That moment of awful truth from which the victim was barely saved fades from his memory. And with the receding of the terrible reality come arguments cloaked in the peculiar morality that flourishes in the rarefied air of the ivory tower. With the passing of the danger, as the waves of time roll over the stark monuments to that moment of extinction, we turn away from the men to whom we rushed for safety, the generals and soldiers who exist in the harsh world of reality, and we begin to listen to the unreal academics, whose frustrations and envy of the men of reality are too often mistaken for spiritual and moral loftiness.

Our combination of weariness and forgetfulness

turns us away from common sense and into the arms of the denizens of the ivory tower, the demagogues and the opportunists. It is at moments like this that we throw away sanity and lose the strength that alone can save us, that alone can enable us to snatch defeat from the jaws of victory.

Perhaps it is common to all peoples, perhaps it is more so with us Jews, this inability to withstand victory. But regardless of the ultimate roots of the problem, the fact remains that five years after 2.6 million Jews, together with their nineteen-year-old state, were saved from extinction, larger and larger numbers of those who were almost slaughtered seek to return again to the moment of truth.

Forgotten are the 1967 pronouncements from Cairo, Damascus, Amman, Beirut, Baghdad, and Fatah. Forgotten are the pledges to throw us into the sea, wash Tel Aviv clean with Jewish blood, and eliminate the "gangster state" of Israel. Forgotten are the insanity of borders that left the coastal strip with its million Jews under the guns of Arab armies just twelve, thirteen, or fifteen kilometers away. Forgotten are the shells that swept into Masaryk Square in Tel Aviv and the Egyptian planes just minutes away from the heartland. Forgotten are our own projections of tens of thousands of soldiers, and perhaps fifty thousand civilians, dead. Forgotten are the borders that left settlements on the Huleh Plain lying naked beneath the Golan Syrian guns, the hills of Ephraim dominating Tel Aviv and its sister cities, the Sinai with its Egyptian land armada within spitting distance of our cities. But forgotten most of all are the hate, the bitter enmity, the solemn pledges of extermination, the schoolbooks with their poisonous venom, the glee and ecstasy of the days of May and early June 1967 when the mobs and potential murderers and rapists were lashing about in an agony of anticipation of the great jihad, the "holy war" that was about to begin. Forgotten is the reality of Arab refusal to recognize a State of Israel that is even one dunam square. Forgotten is the never-changing reality of "Hebronism."

What is "Hebronism"? It is the Arab policy of extermination of the Jew who seeks to live in his own land. It is the reality of that August day of 1929 that saw men, women, and children slaughtered in the streets, homes, and shops of Jewish Hebron. It is the reality of the rape and torture and gouging to death, not of "Zionists," but of yeshiva students and their families, of Ashkenazim and also of Sephardim (the latter who have suddenly become "Jewish Arabs" in the propaganda of Fatah). It is the pogroms of 1920, 1921, 1936–39, and 1947. In short, "Hebronism" is that policy of Arab treatment of Jews that would be the rule for us every day of the week could our enemies only accomplish it. Should we be so insane as to listen to the "doves" among us who would let them do just that?

We are inundated with all kinds of illusions and delusions. Let us return this land or that land and we will have blessed peace. Let us not dare to settle Jews in Eretz Yisroel lest it anger the Arabs and jeopardize blessed peace. Let us make partial and semipartial and total and semitotal agreements that call for compromise and we shall have blessed peace. Let us not move Arabs from the borders and settle Jews there; let us not dare to bomb terrorists lest we hit innocent civilians; let us be "better than they are"—and thus gain blessed peace. Let us recognize the existence of a "Palestine people" despite the refusal of every other Arab country to do so, at a time when they might at last have set up a partial "Palestine" state after 1947. Let us negotiate with our friends the mayors of Gaza and Shehem and Hebron, for they are the solution to the problem of peace. Let us, perhaps, even consider a binational state for the sake of blessed peace. Let us realize that we can reach peace and brotherhood with the Arabs by political concessions and compromises.

It is time for the Jew in Israel to throw away those negative attitudes that he retains from the Galut, the Exile. Chief among these is an unwillingness to look at bitter reality. We may not enjoy hearing it, but the truth is that for many years at least there will not be a sincere de jure peace with the Arabs. It may affect the tender souls of the more spiritually intellectual among us, but one can never attain either peace or security by "compromise" with bitter enemies who have no intentions of compromising with you. Those in Judea, Samaria, and Gaza who do sit down with you because they have no choice, do so only in the hope of getting rid of you as soon as possible. Our enemy, in the long run, is weariness. It is against this enemy that we must struggle. We must gird ourselves with tenacity and determination never to tire of what appears to be a never-ending struggle. For that is what it may very well become: a struggle for Jewish existence and a Jewish state that will never cease to be a struggle; a realization that between us and the Arabs stands a massive barrier that may never be breached; a determination by two peoples to live in a land that at least one will never compromise on. There will grow the weariness of having to send our children to the army without stop. There will grow the weariness of having to leave each year for reserve duty. There will grow the weariness of terrorist attacks on the borders or at the Lod airport or at the Tel Aviv bus terminal. There will, perhaps, again grow the weariness—and the heartbreak—of victims of a new war of attrition. There will grow the weariness of all this, rising to a crescendo with the frustrating cry: "When will it finally end?"

Only the weak succumb to such frustrations; only the weak surrender to Time. A strong and tenacious people know that there may never be an end to the struggle and the sacrifice. But they also look about them and see what their refusal to surrender has accomplished: a state, and today a big one, in much of our Eretz Yisroel; a Jewish state with nearly three million souls and many more to come; the creation of a new and proud Jew. None of these things would have come about had we listened to the intellectual precursors of our modern-day intellectuals and doves. In the name of "peace" there would be no Jewish state; in the name of "morality" there would be no free Jewish nation.

If we hope to survive in the literal sense of the word, let us not succumb to the siren call of easy answers and the tempting promise of "peace." Above all, let us, please, have no illusions. The Arabs intend to wipe us out; we must be strong enough to stop them. The Arabs who live with us in Eretz Yisroel, both those who have done so for twenty-five years and those for just five, do not love us and never will—and one cannot blame them. Let us not play games with them or with ourselves. We give them civil rights and political freedom, but what Jew will ever agree that they should become a majority? What Jew will ever agree to allow Arabs to come in on the same terms as Jews do today under the Law of Return? Israel was formed as a Jewish state. Arabs may have social, economic, and much political equality but, in the end, it is not their state. For the individual Arab we offer much, but for the Arab nation, Israel offers nothing. It is not an Arab state, it is a Jewish state. It came into being because Jews knew that for them there was no hope in a world that thirsted for their bodies and souls. It came into being under the realization that neither king nor republican nor Marxist had the solution to the Jewish problem. That in the end it was the words of the rabbis that proved to be eternally true: "It is a law, it is known that Esau hates Jacob."

And so, Eretz Yisroel, the land of the Jewish people, exists. It can never be anything but that and both we and the Arabs know it. Such a fact allows for few illusions over peace. Perhaps peace will come some day; I, for one, doubt it. Until it does, let us not listen to the delusions that float down to us daily from the ivory tower or from the self-hating Left. Strength and tenacity—they and they alone assure Jewish survival.

A second dangerous illusion that must be dispelled is the one that states: "The policy of the government of Israel not to officially declare Jewish sovereignty over the liberated lands, but nevertheless to hold on to them with a vague promise of readiness to return parts, has proved to be a great success."

This liberal attitude of Israel manifests itself on the one hand by Jewish refusal to allow Jews to settle in any of the West Bank cities, to settle major areas of the region, or to pray without limitation in the second holiest of Jewish shrines, the Cave of the Patriarchs in Hebron. On the other hand, this policy allows Arabs to cross from Jordan and into Jordan, invests money in the lands to raise the economy and lets Arab laborers and tourists visit Israel almost without restriction, collaborates even with Arab leaders whose activities during massacres of Jews are known, and encourages a feeling that some day the Arabs of the West Bank will be independent. This policy, it is said, has proven to be a resounding success as evidenced by the fact that peace and tranquility have been the rule in the lands and a growing trust and closeness has been created.

Stuff and nonsense. The "peaceful" Arab has been so only because he feels beaten and helpless in face of the Jewish army and the excellent Israeli intelligence service with its network of paid informers. If the present situation continues and a new generation of Arabs—not wedded to the soil or the fellah (peasant) mentality it produces—grows up well educated, urbanized, and extreme in its thinking, we will see an end to the idyll.

But far more important are the terrible, negative results of the government's policy. In the short run this policy appears to be a success, but in the long run it can prove to be disastrous. Why?

In the end, the Arabs alone can never hope to overcome Israel. They will need outside help. And the most important help they can get will come from the Israelis themselves. If the greatest of Israeli weapons, confidence in the rightness of our cause, is overcome, if large numbers of Israelis can be led to believe that there is something immoral about Israel's stand on the "Palestine" question, then we will see in Israel a repetition of the United States' Vietnam tragedy, wherein hundreds of thousands of Americans actively participated in attacking government policy and in helping the enemy to win the kind of diplomatic victory it could never have hoped to gain on the field of battle.

The present policy of the Israeli government toward "Palestine" will do exactly that in Israel. If, for example, the West Bank—Judea and Samaria—was really ours, really Jewish, then Israel should have declared so *immediately* after the June 1967 war. Had they done so then, the world would not have opened its mouth to protest. A man who has regained possession of something that he lost, leaps on it and shouts, "This is mine." One who does not do so brings into question his own legitimacy; he raises grave doubts as to whether he is really the rightful owner, and when he then continues to hold on to it, making all kinds of vague offers to return *part* of it to the one who was holding it in the past, he is patently less than genuine.

Such a lesson is not lost on the minds of thousands of young Israelis. They are not fools and neither are they imbued with the attitude of their predecessors that allowed the latter to excuse every seeming inconsistency in the name of the Jewish people. This failure of the Israeli Government to take a resolute stand, this "halting between two opinions," has seriously eroded the confidence in the policies and morality of their own state of more youth than the government would like to admit. This is the most dangerous thing that can happen to a nation and its consequences, as we well know, can be disastrous.

If we wish to avoid a terrible rise in mistrust of the government by our young; if we want to prevent the rise of a conviction among various sectors of our population that we are indeed a conquering and robbing army; if we wish to make it very clear to any budding Arab nationalists that no amount of pressure will avail them anything since we do not intend to leave; if we hope to keep secure borders; if we want to shut off the protests of the hypocritical world; above all, if we intend to realize the enormous miracle and promise of Jewish renaissance and return to historic Eretz Yisroel—then the present policy of trickery, ruse, and dishonesty must be abandoned.

In its place a new, honest and direct policy must be implemented that consists of: (1) immediate permission for Jewish settlement in every part of the liberated lands, city and countryside; (2) crash programs for immediate Jewish settlement directly in the heart of major cities—such as Hebron, Shehem, Jericho, Gaza, and Ramallah—that will direct new immigration into these areas and the creation of western-style cities with western capital to attract western immigrants. In a word, the liberated lands must be speedily and immediately re-Judaized.

This, in brief, is what must be done to bury the illusions concerning the territory and population of the liberated lands as well as the general Arab-Israeli

OUR CHALLENGE   38

conflict. There remain, however, other illusions concerning one other aspect of the Jewish-Arab dispute: the Arabs of the State of Israel within the pre-1967 borders.

These Arabs are, of course, a part of the general Israel-Arab struggle, and even if there were no outside Arabs to contend with, they would pose a tremendous problem in themselves. As a minority, and a growing one, that lives in our midst as part of the state and yet not quite part of it, they will in the years to come become a problem that will cause severe internal conflict and strike at the very roots of the state. Concerning them, just as with the general Arab-Israel dispute, we have begun to cherish dangerous illusions.

We must begin to disabuse ourselves of the illusion that the demon of Arab demography will be disposed of by getting rid of the lands that hold a million post-June-1967 Arabs. I put it to one and all that the problem of Arab numbers and an ever-growing Arab minority will not be disposed of by disposing of the territories, and that this gnawing problem exists in the form of the Arabs of that part of Israel that existed *before* 1967. Indeed, I hasten to add, the Arabs within what is known as "the Green line" will pose a far more dangerous and explosive threat to Israel than those of Hebron and Gaza. What I am really saying is that the signing of a peace treaty with the Arabs, the setting up of a "Palestine" state that is free and independent, the recognition of Israel by the Arabs—all these impossible dreams, even if they were fulfilled, would still leave Israel with an Arab time bomb that could blow up the state and bring to life all the problems we thought were solved.

Let us assume that a peace will somehow be achieved and all the "outside" Arabs plus those in their own new "Palestine" state will accept Israel. What will happen is that Israel will not have been freed of an Arab nationalist problem. It will not have been freed of an Arab population problem. It will not have been freed of a large body that hates the Jewish majority and the Jewish state and seeks its destruction or at least its total overhaul and change of identity. All of these problems will remain in the form of the Israeli Arabs. Concerning these Arabs, we have begun to believe all kinds of myths.

Thus our third dangerous illusion: "The way to reach peace and understanding between Jew and Arab is to raise the Arab standard of living and create a new generation of educated Arabs. Already, Israel has succeeded in raising the living standards of its own Arabs to the point where they are the highest in the Arab world and where more and more Arabs enter high schools and universities each year. If this continues there is hope of bridging the Arab-Israel gap."

No nationalist was ever bought by an indoor toilet and electricity in his home. And that is exactly what those who preach peace through materialism are doing. They are buying, or attempting to buy, the Arab nationalist and his love and pride in nationhood and state. Such an attempt is as immoral as it is self-defeating. What the "moderates" and the "compromisers" do not realize is that the Arab nationalist is as committed to his own people and to what he considers his own land as the Jews of Israel are to theirs. The Western colonialists who sincerely and honestly believed that they were benefitting the Asians and Africans whom they ruled, found that their arguments fell on deaf ears of native peoples who preferred poverty with independence to high living standards under foreign rule. Why should we expect the Arabs to be any different? Why should they not have the same pride that Israelis expect their children to have?

Certainly with this present generation, mostly illiterate peasants, large numbers can be "bribed." But in the years to come, as the sons of the peasants become educated nationalists and extremists, they will contemptuously reject our "favors." No, let us not deceive ourselves into believing that by raising the Arab living standards we will win his peace and friendship.

The illusions concerning education are even more incomprehensible. Has not history shown a hundred times over that it is precisely the educated intellectuals who are the most nationalistic and extreme? It is not the fellah, the Arab peasant, who is the danger to peace with Israel, but rather his son who goes to high school and from there to the university. He, who has economic opportunities that were undreamed of by his father, will not be "grateful" to the Jew for allowing him to enter new worlds. Quite the contrary.

The university Arab sits and reads of the great nationalist movements of history, demands the same for his own people and land, acquires the knowledge, sophistication, and tools of leadership and becomes the most extreme, the most nationalist, and the most talented of the Arabs. Peace and understanding from the university Arabs? Anything but.

And despite this most elementary lesson, there are those in the government who are able to speak about and find funds for an Arab university. Money for the poverty areas of Israel, we do not have. Money to meet the communal gap, we are told, is simply nonexistent. But funds to finance a school for Arab nationalists, extremist leaders who will lead the battle for our destruction, suddenly appear. We Jews are indeed a strange people.

There is another aspect of the problem that we ignore at our peril. It is not only the Arab of the lands liberated in 1967 who conceives of himself as a "Palestinian" and who believes that the Jews have stolen his homeland. The Arab who lived in pre-1967 Israel, the one who is granted Israeli citizenship and has been an Israel citizen since 1948, the free and equal Arab citizen of the Jewish state thinks exactly the same way. And if he is a *young* Arab, who was born after Israel came into being and lived his whole life under Israeli sovereignty, he feels even more strongly about it.

He does not conceive of himself as part of the state: he is an Arab, not a Jew; a "Palestinian," not an Israeli. He does not feel he owes loyalty to his government; he does not look upon it as *his* government. He resents and hates the Jewish majority. He is at heart as strong a "Palestinian" and Arab nationalist as the West Bank Arab, and because of guilt feelings engendered by his acquiescence in Israeli citizenship, he is a potentially greater and more dangerous one. He wants to *prove* his Arabism. He rejects categorically the constant assertion by various government officials that the Israeli Arab is an equal citizen of the state.

And here we come to the final illusion: "The Israeli Arab is equal to the Israeli Jew in the Jewish state."

So long as Israel remains the Jewish state, and that

is its reason for being; so long as Israel is the fulfillment of the Zionist dream, a homeland for the Jewish people where they can be a majority and plan their own destiny; so long as there is a Law of Return, which grants every Jew (not Arab) automatic citizenship upon request, precisely in order to assure a Jewish majority—the Arab in Israel will never be as equal as the Jew. It will always be the *Jewish* state, the state of the Jew, not the Arab.

All the "liberals," "progressives," and leftists may grind their teeth, but if they believe in Zionism, in whatever shape, and in a Jewish state, they must accept this fact. No amount of dialectics or sophistry will make it vanish. A Jewish state means that there is an inherent difference between the Jewish citizen and the Arab one.

And why not? If the purpose of moving large numbers of Jews to Israel was not for the purpose of setting up a Jewish state with a permanent Jewish majority, why leave New York City with its two million Jews, or the Soviet Union with its three million? A large Jewish minority is not the answer that Zionism proposed to the question of anti-Semitism. We have had large Jewish minorities in the past and they have availed us nothing. A large ghetto is still a ghetto, not a Jewish state. Israel was conceived as a *Jewish* state, a Jewish *majority* state. It was conceived as the one home of the Jewish people just as every nation has its home with its majority. For this concept, there is no need to apologize.

But it does present us with a fact that the "progressive" and the Left always pass over in embarrassment. That fact is that the Arab in Israel may be a citizen, he

The Chosen Land 43

may be given equal opportunities in education and employment, but he is doomed to a minority role because he is an Arab in a Jewish state. And from this flows the inescapable resentment on the part of any minority, which is compounded by the Arab's belief that the state is really his, and that he should be the majority.

It is no solution to this problem to seek a resolution of the Arab's identity crisis. The Arab cannot combine his Arab nationalism with living in a Jewish, not Arab, state. The growing number of educated Israeli Arabs, those entering secondary schools and universities, will never constitute a more moderate and compromising Arab minority. Precisely the opposite. Every example of history shows that revolutionaries come not from the numb, dumb peasant and oppressed classes but from the intellectual middle or upper classes, or the sons of the oppressed classes who have escaped into the rarified atmosphere of the university. It is the new, educated Arab generation that is infinitely more dangerous, that is unwilling to accept its status as a something less than first class citizen and that will resort to ever-growing protest and revolts.

What is more, the growing rootlessness and lack of Jewish values among Israeli Jewish youth is bound to lead to a condition, similar to that in the United States and almost every western country, wherein "majority" intellectuals, driven by their lack of values to a neurotic self-hate and the need to attack the parental and state Establishment, will latch on to the "oppressed" Arab as a means to channel their own destructive impulses. Exactly as in the United States, intellectual Jewish youth will find themselves a cause, the "persecuted" Arabs, and give them (the Arabs) the thing they most lacked to make their revolt meaningful: majority leadership. A minority can never win against a determined majority, but when that majority is divided, when its youth and intellectuals are driven by doubt, self-hate and mistrust of their own government, then the conditions are ripe for revolt, tension, and anarchy.

What we will see as the years pass is the growth of educated Arabs whose nationalism will be bitter and extreme. We will also see a corresponding growth of Arabs whose intellectual and educational achievements will not find an appropriate occupational outlet, with many hundreds unable to find the professional and political jobs their ambitions demand. We will see a society where most of the laboring jobs are Arab and the better ones Jewish. This will lead to increasing frustration, tension, boldness, civil disobedience, demonstrations, protests, riots, and revolt. Growing numbers of young Jews will actively support these Arabs; the Israeli Left, from the Moscow-puppet Rakach party to the schizophrenic Mapam, will aid them politically; and there will be created conditions similar to those in the United States civil rights revolt—which has only begun and which will yet see warfare in the streets.

Once again, none of this is strange or bizarre. There has never been an instance of two peoples, both sizable and both fully believing that the land is theirs, which have managed to permanently coexist in that same land. Whether in Northern Ireland, India, Quebec, Yugoslavia, Cyprus, or even Belgium, grave differences in nationality, race, religion, or language have created iron curtains between the groups involved. How much more so in the case of the Jews and Arabs of Israel, where all the above differences exist against a background of hate and war.

The revolutionary Left, liberals of all kinds, and anti-Semites in general will seize upon the "plight" of the Arabs to raise an international hue and cry, to organize worldwide protests and support on behalf of the Arabs. Their efforts will hurt, to an as yet unknown degree, financial support for Israel, both from foreign governments as well as private supporters—including Jews.

These axioms that I have outlined make up a scenario. What emerges is an unpleasant realization that Israel faces a terrible crisis that threatens her as no other crisis in the past. I have not even touched upon the growing intermarriage rate between Jews and Arabs, a phenomenon that may not bother "liberals" but that spells doom for Jews just as surely as the pogroms that take their physical lives.

What is the solution? Certainly not to ignore the problem. Certainly not to persuade ourselves that it does not exist or that it is not as bad as some people make it out to be or that it will get better or that it will eventually disappear of its own accord. Not by illusions or patently impossible brotherhood hopes will this problem be solved.

Illusions will not save the Israelis; good, hard common sense will. Certainly every effort must be made to increase the Jewish population of Israel through a crisis approach to immigration and strenuous efforts to raise the Jewish birth rate. But at least equally as important is the need to find some way to reduce the Arab minority. And here we refer both to the Arabs who are Israeli citizens as well as to the inhabitants of the liberated territories.

The best partial solution, the most humane in the long run, and the safest for the Jews is an effort to separate the Arab minority from the Jewish majority by a planned and well-funded emigration of Arabs from Israel. I speak here of the idea for an urgent creation of an Emigration Fund for Peace (Keren Hegira Imaan ha-Shalom) and I immediately point out that I refer only to a voluntary one, through the free choice and determination of individual Arabs.

Naturally, the extremist, the proud nationalist will not leave, but many, many other thousands will. If it can be pointed out to the Arabs that Jewish majority rule will never be displaced and that they are being offered an opportunity that, most likely, will never be theirs again—to begin new lives in the West—the chances are excellent that they will leave. What population transfers created for Greeks and Turks, Indians and Pakistanis, and Sudetan Germans, can be repeated here.

The most important obstacle is, of course, the small but vocal group of rootless and frustrated neo-intellectuals who will be the first to attack the plan and smear it with all kinds of labels. Yet it is up to those who love the Jewish people and state and hope to save them both from a disastrous crisis, to ignore the false prophets of false and ignorant "liberalism" and to make this plan a

The Chosen Land 47

reality. Integration is not always the answer, although it is not always *not* the answer. In this case, an attempt to integrate the Arabs of Israel can be successful only at the price of a unique Jewish state, and without the willingness to pay that price it is an exercise in dangerous futility. Let us then ignore those who are "overly righteous." Let us speak of the need for a private body of wealthy and influential Jews to establish an emigration fund with an *initial* capitalization of at least twenty million dollars. Such money could be raised with comparative ease if wealthy western Jewry would be quietly but firmly persuaded by the Israeli government that this fund is vital to her interests and welfare.

These same people should also begin the task of contacting governments of states that are underpopulated or in need of manpower to see exactly how many visas they are willing to allocate both for their own self-interest as well as for the purpose of defusing the time bomb that is the Arab population of the Land of Israel. Governments should also be discreetly asked how much they would be willing to contribute to this fund, which would do more to solve the Middle East problem than all the United Nations plans yet created.

A careful table should be drawn up, based on living conditions in different countries and the size of families, to ascertain how much should be allotted to individuals and families that would wish to emigrate.

With a fund of money, with visas, with exact charts, the Arabs—and here I stress that this plan would be offered to both the Arabs of pre-1967 Israel and those of the liberated lands—would then be approached and offered a sizable sum (more than enough to begin a new life) to emigrate to the country of their choice (within the list of states that has agreed to take them in). A number of Arab countries might agree to take in skilled labor with capital; this would certainly be preferable to emigration to non-Arab countries.

Jews in the receiving countries should be enlisted to see about jobs and housing for the emigrating Arabs, and schools to teach these Arabs the skills that are needed in the new lands should be funded and set up either in Israel or in the country of emigration.

Will many Arabs leave? I believe that, if given the monetary incentive and promise of a new life free from the eternal threat of hatred and minority status, many will. Whatever the number, Israel will benefit from even that limited emigration. Bear in mind the extraordinarily high birthrate of the Arabs of Israel and that each one who leaves takes with him many future Arabs. It is a plan that is worth trying and that promises blessings for the Jewish state. Above all it is an answer worthy of the most serious thought because of the potential disaster inherent in the lack of an answer.

A brief comment on criticism of the plan from responsible circles, particularly within the government, criticism that condemns the plan for "offending" the Arabs and harming "friendly relations" between them and the Jews. It is difficult to comprehend a cabinet and a ruling party that make such statements, which contain more than a little contradiction. One simply cannot understand those leading government officials who publicly call for the return of parts of the liberated lands on the grounds that they do not "want too many Arabs," and then condemn others for proposing an emigration plan. Do we really think that such a plan would offend the Arabs and make relations difficult? If so, what in the world do we think an Israeli Arab feels when he hears his prime minister, finance minister, foreign minister, deputy premier, and other assorted Laborites talk about the danger of too many Arabs in a Jewish state? Do we really think we make friends and influence people that way?

The difference between the advocates and the opponents of the plan is that one group plays games with the Arabs and tries to fool them while the other tells the truth. Labor wants to get rid of the Arabs by giving back Jewish land; we want to try to keep Eretz Yisroel and find some means to convince the Arabs to leave.

What of those who will not leave? They will certainly be the majority, so that under any circumstances the resources and brains of the state must be mobilized to increase the numbers of Jews and the proportion of Jews to Arabs, as well as finding some means whereby the Arabs of the territories will not opt for Israeli citizenship. Let us again repeat that there are two problems posed by the Arabs within Eretz Yisroel. One is the fact of their existence within the borders as a large, potentially dissident and seditious minority. The second is their potential political and electorate power that could threaten the Jewish hegemony of the Jewish state. Both problems could be eased by emigration, but even if large numbers choose to remain, the second problem can still be met and modified.

OUR CHALLENGE 50

Those Arabs who remain within the Land of Israel, both pre-1967 and in the liberated lands, pose a politically demographic threat. The threat must be met not by returning land that is sacred and Jewish and whose return would pose a security threat of catastrophic proportions, but by other means. Certainly, nothing can be done to limit the rights of those Arabs who are already Israeli citizens, or their children. But the Arab population of the liberated lands that should and must be made part of Eretz Yisroel can be politically neutralized.

First, it should be made clear that the incorporation of the territories into Israel will not bring with it automatic citizenship and that the non-Jews there will be treated exactly as if they were non-Jews from some other area coming into Israel. That is, that they must apply for citizenship which will be given to them after the regular five-year wait.

At the end of that time, the applicant must repeat his intention of becoming a citizen and swearing loyalty to the State of Israel. Notice of such intention and declaration will be printed in three Arab newspapers for two consecutive weeks. The intent here is clearly to discourage the Arab from asking for citizenship.

At the same time, the government should make a definite offer to all territorial residents that those who opt for noncitizenship will be automatically freed from national taxes, as well as pushing for a mass program of birth-control education and "liberating" literature for Arab women. All efforts to combine education that will reduce the high Arab birthrate with government incentives aimed at raising the Jewish birthrate are vital in the demographic war.

In addition, every conceivable Jewish resource must go into the effort to increase Aliya, Jewish immigration, to mass proportions. This is an absolute necessity not only for the Jews of the Galut themselves, but also for those in Israel. The infusion of two million and more Jews into the state assures us a political majority, whatever the numbers of Arabs. Furthermore, there is an extraordinary difference between the small population we have today and a large Jewish state of five million Jews. One does not speak so glibly of wiping out or dismantling such a state. Because of this, one cannot demand too strongly that Israeli efforts toward maximum Aliya through all possible means be expanded to the utmost, regardless of the reactions of any group or government.

On the one hand, efforts to reduce the Arab birthrate, population, and political power; on the other, attempts at raising the number of Jews: both are essential to the creation of a maximum Jewish state that will live and thrive, free from threats of annihilation and from internal efforts at sedition and anarchy.

The overall Arab-Israel problem will not be solved for decades. Indeed, it may never be solved. This holds true also for the Jewish-Arab problem *within* Israel. For those who ask, "but what will the end be?" the mature answer is that ultimately the Messiah will come and, until then, who knows? Besides, who ever said there *must* be a solution? Some problems have remained unsolved for centuries despite many honest efforts to solve them. What we must *not* do is allow our impatience and weariness to push us into a false solution that will lead to disaster. We are obligated to find as much of a *real* solution as is possible.

The Arabs and Jews of Israel and the Middle East may never live in true peace together. Foolish idealism is no substitute for true idealism or even for any kind of reality. What is needed is a reaffirmation of the age-old faith in "the destiny of Israel which will not prove faithless" and a determined, realistic policy aimed at the most important of all Jewish goals—Jewish survival.

Let us not be frightened into guilt feelings and into a retreat from common sense, self-preservation, and our Jewish destiny by the attacks of the lovers of "peace." Those who advocate Jewish self-preservation are just as anxious for peace as the confused and strident shouters on the Left. Their wives and children face the same threat and their Jewish gabardine is just as legitimate as the cloak of the self-proclaimed "peace-seekers."

The difference is that the Jewish nationalist lives with reality, not illusion. He had faith in the Jewish destiny, the Almighty's promise and the strong Jewish hand that brings the miraculous to reality. He knows that the Almighty and Jewish destiny will not desert the Jew, but he knows that success is conditioned on his own efforts at formulating and carrying out a realistic and bold Jewish policy.

In the end, we will be fortunate in that, with the most foolish and myopic of intentions, we will be unable to destroy ourselves and the Almighty will save us from the fruits of our own folly. We have reached that stage in Jewish history and destiny where it is ordained that the Jewish return to the homeland will be permanent, maximum, and glorious. No assortment of timid, fearful, and tiny politicians can undo this. What they can do, however, is cost us great amounts of tragedy in the form of human suffering and lost opportunities. They can retard the salvation and make us pay heavily. In the end, however, the redemption will out, for this is the determination of divine providence.

3

The Chosen People: Questions

It was a week after the revelation that a number of young Jews had been arrested and accused of being part of a Syrian spy ring. The news that a number of young Jews, sabras, and one from a kibbutz, were accused of acting against the Jewish state for ideological reasons, led the Prime Minister of Israel to say: "I was surprised. A week ago I would have sworn that such a thing could not happen."

There were others, too, who were surprised, in fact

astounded. But *they* were astounded at the surprise of the Prime Minister that indicated so much lack of awareness at what is happening today among the golden youth, the *noar zahav.*

We wallow in our illusions. "There can be no large-scale Israeli youth rebellion," we say, "as there is in the West, against Jewish ties, against the concept that Jews are all one people whose Jewishness takes precedence even over 'Israeli-ness.' There can be no quarrel with the argument that the destiny of each Jew is within that indivisible, world Jewish framework, that the fate of all Jews is the fate and obligation of the Israeli. There can be no rejection of Zionism, the belief in one, indivisible Jewish people and the destiny of the Jew perceived as within this context of people and land. There can be no mass flirting with a Left that rejects nationalism for class struggle and a universal world that buries Judaism as both a faith and people. There can be no massive crime, violence, and drug problem; there can be no mass retreat from moral standards; there can be no hedonistic search for individual pleasure; there can be no rejection of 'parochialism,' of nationalism and Jewishness, and no preaching of the brotherhood of all revolutionaries (including Palestinians) against imperialism—including Zionism. There can be no 'progressive' thinking that will see nothing wrong with intermarriage, for ours are golden youth, and if we see a few disturbing spots here and there, have no fear—they will go away as soon as there is a war with the Arabs. Ours, after all, are *noar zahav.*"

But of course we deceive ourselves, just as Jews

(or perhaps all humans) always do when they prefer not to think about unpleasant things and a thousand times more so when the unpleasantness hovers about a subject very dear to them. We delude ourselves and pooh-pooh those who warn us. It can't happen here! That which afflicted modern, western Jewish youth everywhere else in the world cannot happen here! We Israelis, who so superciliously mock the American Jew for parroting these words and not learning from the physical lesson of Germany, merrily repeat the same foolishness in reference to the spiritual and national disaster that faces our people, in the de-Judaization of Israeli youth. It is, by far, the most serious problem facing the Jewish state, far more serious than Arabs, or borders, or economics.

Of course it can happen here, and indeed it is happening. Too many parents, teachers, comfortable businessmen, and old-time Zionist ideologists who created this youth neither know what is going on nor want to know. It is so much more pleasant and reassuring not to look too deeply into the warnings of the "eternal pessimists"—particularly if they have not been in the country for forty years, are not part of the Israeli "Mayflower" set, are only "newcomers" who should live here for twenty years before venturing an opinion.

Not so very long ago in the United States there was also a *noar zahav;* do not think that the madness of drugs, infantile campus Leftism, anarchy of values, and irrational attacks on the state were always part of the American scene. As one who was born in the United States, one who lived there, studied there, was part of it, and saw it change, I can testify to what once was.

What once was—and barely ten years ago at that—was a youth exactly as apathetic as Israeli youth; that hardly ever dreamed of questioning their loyalty to and confidence in their country and government; to whom the idea of cursing the president was obscenely foreign; to whom the flag was a thing before which one stood reverently and pledged allegiance; to whom the army was the staunch defender, not only of their own lives and safety, but of freedom and liberty throughout the world; to whom communism was an evil to be devoutly fought; to whom drugs and license were things one read of but never remotely practiced. In short, an American world of quiet, patriotic, conservative, and apathetic youth.

Within a decade that world turned upside down, before the startled eyes of parents, educators, and comfortable citizens who stared in bewilderment at the wild revolution and stammered the eternal question: "Where did we go wrong?"

The answers would fill volumes, but we can touch upon one of them. America went wrong when it ignored and underestimated the power of the first small groups of revolutionaries (whether political or social) to win the minds of vast numbers of their peers, who had been given an American life devoid of real values. America which measures everything in terms of numbers laughed at the tiny Left that began to preach its creed on campuses and in schools. "How many members have they got?" may be the last words that the silent majority will be able to express in freedom. America went wrong when it forgot that the physical law that nature abhors a vacuum, that something must fill it, finds its application in the life of man also. America saw the rise of the cults and leftists and refused to meet the challenge by setting up ideas and groups to move in and fill the ideological and moral vacuum. Something else did.

For the American Jew, there was not only a loss of a child as far as American values were concerned. With the second American revolution went, too, the Judaism he had bequeathed to that child. The Judaism of his temple and his UJA and his Bar Mitzvah and his lox and his Miami Beach and his B'nai B'rith also went the way of the old as his child nonchalantly cast off all vestiges of the Judaism that his parents had so carefully diluted and "modernized." That which his father had bankrupted the son cheerfully jettisoned.

And the American Jewish tragedy began with conditions very similar to those today in Israel. For one who was there, events here are the repetition of a bad dream, once escaped. Here, too, in the "better" high schools, "better" neighborhoods, and in the universities, small groups of more sensitive, more consciously confused, more restive youth are coming to grips with the irrelevance and boredom of their lives. Here, too, growing numbers of frustrated, embittered, and rebellious writers, intellectuals, and professors are beginning to play the role of spokesmen for the "oppressed" and to poison the minds of naive and impressionable students and followers. Here, too, freedom and growing affluence have created a dissatisfied and searching youth that rejects the vapid values of parents and society and that despises both for their lack of guidance. Here, too, small groups of extremists spring up and promise exciting worlds of ideas and new "religions" that can fill the spiritual emptiness in a youth whose parents exchanged their Judaism for a material pottage of lentils. Here, too, we see the first budding of the attempts to flee from unpleasant and difficult reality through sex and drugs. And here, too, we see the first—but hardly the last—tentative assaults on all the sacred cows that were once above the slightest criticism: Zionism, the army, and the state itself.

So let us here, in Israel, avoid the blindness of those in the Exile. Let us realize that if there is an anti-Zionist, Marxist Matzpen movement; if there are groups that preach that there are too many links with the past and that we must cast adrift our Jewishness for a kind of "Israeli-ness" that will find its acceptable niche within the nations of the Middle East; if there are groups that tell our youth that we have stolen the land, and oppressed the Palestinians; if there are people who call Ashkenazim the deadly enemies of the Sephardim; if there are students who are "sick of hearing about" the Holocaust and the *shtetl;* and if there are those who want to speak about a Jewish nationalism without a religion (consider the "Jewish nationalist of the Christian faith") and others who wish to reject the concept of a Jewish nationality at all ("Let the Galut Jew remain a Jew; we are Israelis")—then there is a danger, and more young Israeli Jews than we care to think about are infected with it. And let us not astonish the world by statements of astonishment at the disclosure of the existence of Jewish spies. Let us recognize that the problem of

Jewish youth and their values—or lack of values—is the most urgent one facing us today and that the solution of all our other problems depends on whether we solve it or not. There is a disease afflicting our youth today and we must remedy it.

The origin of the disease is not difficult to understand. The Israeli youth, like his Galut counterpart, *is not sure who he is.* All the Zionism and Jewish nationalism that was going to make him a new, proud, free Jew, all the dreams of the Brenners and Berdechevskis and Ben Gurions, have a flat taste of ashes today. The sabra (native-born Israeli) does not possess the nostalgia for the Galut with its Judaism that made David Ben Gurion the Zionist Jew he is (whether the Old Man cares to admit it or not; whether he cares to consider that his philosophy that retains the Jewish national quality is really only a product of environmental nostalgia.) The sabra never knew the Galut, never had the anti-Semite give him a beating and a negative reason for being a Jew. He looks at the "foreign" Jews, his brothers, who come to visit his land with their strange languages and different habits. He scratches his new Jewish head, asking, "What am I?" His religion long since went the way of all "antiquities" and in this he was encouraged by the teaching and examples of his elders. But the tragedy of the loss of Torah and tradition does not end only with the absolute loss of truth that the Torah represents. The tragedy is compounded by the massive error of the secularist nationalists who thought that their pure Jewish nationalism could be handed down to the next generation intact. Their error is glaringly revealed in the sabra who asks, "Who am I? What am I?"

The Chosen People: Questions

It is a question asked by millions both in Israel and in the Galut. Until some hundred and fifty years ago, the Jews of the world knew exactly what they were, and more important, why they were. It was this that allowed them to preserve both their sanity and existence in a mad, cruel world that sucked their blood and sought their extinction. A nation—or individual—that understands its framework, its purpose on earth, and its reason for existence will be normal and prepared to come to grips with life. One who has roots and direction will find his place in this world and march purposefully forward with a clear mind and an understanding heart.

But a man or a people that has no goal or for whom purpose in being is unclear and filled with doubt, whose life becomes a tortuous nightmare of searching ever more desperately and irrationally for elusive answers, is doomed to a life of failure, frustration, and waste.

The Jew of ancient and medieval times may have been a man who suffered greatly and for whom life was a series of agonizing persecutions, pogroms, and poverty, but he knew who he was, from whence he came, and where he was going, and it was this that gave him strength to continue and the sure knowledge that eventual victory would be his. What did the Jew know? What was his reason for being? How did he define himself and his place within the framework of existence? There was nothing puzzling or new in this definition. It was one that was quite old—exactly as old as the Revelation at Sinai:

The Jew knew that he was a member of a unique and separate people, divinely chosen at Sinai as a religio-nation, transcending the foolishness and dangers of shallow secular nationalism that merely divides without raising up. He knew that G-d had chosen the Jewish people to learn, uphold, and teach to his children the divine wisdom of Torah, and that the divine destiny of the Jewish people was to realize its greatness and its exclusiveness, to remain separate from the nations lest it assimilate and lose its divine uniqueness, and to return to the homeland of Eretz Yisroel, there to rebuild an independent, truly Jewish state that would be a model society for mankind.

In this definition there were no agonizing questions over whether the Jews were a nation or religion; over the relationship between one Jew and another, regardless of their citizenship; over who was a Jew; over the relationship between Jew and gentile; over universalism, assimilation, Reform, Diaspora nationalism, or socialist class struggle. All Jews were brothers and part of one religio-nation. Religion and nation constituted one entity, and there was no Jew who was not simultaneously part of the same religion and nation. Above all, there was a common Jewish destiny, and the gentile, with his separate ways and denial of Judaism, was separate and apart from it.

With the coming of the Emancipation and the literal and figurative collapse of the ghetto, the definition changed. It changed because numbers of Jews who sensed material opportunities and saw the dim light of freedom and equality in the society of nations understood (and quite correctly) that with such a Jewish definition as their fathers and ancestors had carried, assimilation and integration into the gentile world was impossible. And so, lubricated by the desire for integration and assimilation, the Mendelssohns and Friedlanders and Furtados and Riessers cast away the first part of the mighty, ancient definitions of Jew: The Jew was no longer a member of a nation: he no longer longed for a Zion in the Middle East. *Here* was Zion (and "here" was Hamburg or Paris or Amsterdam or London or Charleston, South Carolina). The dream of freedom and equal opportunity broke down the definition of the exclusiveness of the Jew, and the broken definition hastened immeasurably the spiritual destruction of the German or French or what-have-you of "Mosaic persuasion."

Religion was the next Jewish sacrifice on the altar of assimilation. Reform Judaism emasculated the religion as, in its zeal to assure the total death of the Jews as a nation, it eliminated every reference to a return to Zion in Eretz Yisroel or to a redemption from a Galut that it denied it was in. And along with the death of the national aspects of Judaism came the inevitable changes that made it more *acceptable* to the Christian. The mortal inferiority complex that plagued the Jews of the Emancipation; the morbid self-hatred that produced mass flights to baptism on the part of people like Mendelssohn's daughter Dorothea, Rahel Levin, and Heinrich Heine, also drove emancipated Jewry to produce "temples" and a religion close enough to Christianity to avoid invidious comparison. Not only was Zion amputated from the Jewish articles of faith, but the articles themselves received a thorough emasculation. Some, indeed, may have acted from higher motives, but the inescapable fact is that the change from synagogue to temple, from traditional services to organs, ministerial robes, mixed pews, women in minyans, and the like was due to the drive to be "like unto the goyim."

It goes without saying that the emasculation could not have taken place without the denial of the *amud ha-ymini,* the right-hand pillar upon which Judaism always stood and which was correctly understood as being the sole logical and rational support for exclusive existence. The sweeping changes made by the men of the Emancipation and Enlightenment could have come about only if the Judaism they amputated was also merely a product of men. A Judaism that was G-d given and divinely handed down, a Judaism based upon the Revelation of the Almighty to his people was not a thing that even the great men of the nineteenth-century West could trifle with. And so Revelation as a doctrine in Judaism was quietly and respectfully buried. To be sure, most of the reformers could not screw up their courage to say so unequivocably (in their denial of G-d they were not quite able to be men). Such reformers played with a Revelation that was not quite that; with a G-d who (in some mysterious way neither they nor anyone else could ever explain) reveals himself constantly to all reformers; with a religion that was divine in its finite humanness.

Of course, such theological fraud could be accepted by those who created it for their own peace of mind, but could never stand the slightest test of intellectual honesty and anger—such as displayed in our time by the young, who see through such nonsense with little difficulty. Little wonder that neither the nineteenth-century Reform *pilpul* (so much more tortuous than the yeshiva brand the modernists gleefully mocked) or the incredible religious permutations of our time (G-d as the "power that makes for salvation," G-d as a "functional concept") left new generations either cold or contemptuous. Judaism without Revelation, without a special, unique reason for Jewish teachings and religion, left its adherents without a special, unique reason for cleaving to particularism, for being a Jew. All the further agonizing and desperate answers—that Judaism is unique in its ethical monotheism and its call for social justice— serve only to raise millions of young Jewish eyebrows. Their owners know that Christian rebels, Marxists, Third World types, ethical culturists, and all kinds of uncircumcized people shout "ethics" and "peace" quite as loudly as the local temple rabbi and Socialist-Zionist Histadrut boss.

Ethical monotheism? Social justice? Peace? Brotherhood? Is that all there is? Is that all there is to being Jewish? If that is all there is, then let us rather be humans, part of that great universal brotherhood of men who ignore foolish and dangerous artificial divisions such as nationalism and religion, and concentrate on building one happy world. This is the salvation of humanity and the Jew; this is the solution to the "Jewish problem."

Indeed, this is precisely the path that the assimilationists took. Heine, in his early escape from his people and faith, could exult: "And what is the great task of our day? It is emancipation. Not simply the emancipation of the Irish, the Greeks, Frankfort Jews, West

Indian blacks and all such oppressed peoples, but the emancipation of the whole world. . . ."

Heine's words were echoed by an American Jewish intellectual more than a hundred years later: "A Jew can best fill his moral obligations not by becoming especially involved in 'the Jewish community' . . . but by joining the community of radical political action. . . . For the commitment to broaden the contours of human freedom and justice must take precedence over everything else; to me, the Jewish tradition has no meaning except when it is incident to that greater tradition." Painful words for the "good" Jew to hear? No doubt, but inexorably logical and following from the death of Judaism as a unique faith with a clear reason for a separate existence.

How pitiful the efforts by the Reformers then—and now—to find some kind of Jewish raison d'être! How sad their attempt to palely resurrect the once bold and unashamed tradition of a Chosen People. From an uncomplicated concept of a special, separate, and unique nation, the enlightened now had to resort to all manner of sophistry and sophistication. We are now chosen to wander among the goyim (rather than build our own state), and raise them up to our level (and one can imagine how the poor goyim simply fell all over themselves with delight at being told this). We were chosen to reform their institutions (through Liberalism? Marxism? Rationalism?) and their ideas. How the indigenous natives enjoy strangers—who really mean to benefit them—coming to them to change their way of life!

Little wonder that this emasculation begat yet another natural progeny—socialism. When the stunning and breathtaking cry to the workers of the world to unite shattered the oppressive heavens of Eastern Europe, is it any wonder that a people who had been subjected to the Emancipation's trumpeting of self-hate responded? If the Russian-Jewish newspaper *Razvet* began to batter down traditional Jewish life by stating that "our motherland is Russia. And just as her air is ours, so too, must her language be ours"; and if the *maskilim* heaped dung upon Judaism and Jewry; if Gordon could tell his people to "be a Jew at home and a man in the street"—then surely the answer of the young Jew upon being told that "Jew" and "man" were mutually exclusive, was to choose to be a "man" both in the street and at home. And if Levanda could write in his childish novel: "My heart tells me that in time the Russians will come to love us. We will make them love us. How? By our own love," then the throwing off of all the "withered leaves" (to quote Lilienblum) and the "absurdities" (Gordon) was a thing that the youth was prepared to do—in a more direct and more honest manner then the *maskilim* dared contemplate.

Socialism, whether the "Jewish" kind of Kremer and Medem's Bund or the "general" kind that saw enough Jews flock to the Bolsheviks and Mensheviks to make *minyanim* (quorums) at every committee meeting, was yet another logical outcome of the death of the uniqueness of the Jew, of the shattering of his nationalism and the emasculation of his religion. What is so inexplicable about the words of a Jewish May Day orator in the halcyon year of 1892: "We Jews repudiate all our national holidays and fantasies which are useless for human society. We link ourselves up with armies of Socialism and adopt their holidays. . . ."

Nothing inexplicable. Certainly it is far more logical than the Sabbaths and holidays of the Jew in his Reform or Conservative temple, when the Torah scroll is raised and all shout: "And this is the Torah that Moses set before the Children of Israel, by word of G-d through Moses," while steadfastly "knowing" that every word is a lie.

And then came secular Zionism: Jewish nationalism whose purpose was to create a "normal" people like all others, to save the Jew.

The Zionist fathers of the nation have eaten the sour grapes of secular nationalism and their sabra children's ideological teeth are set on edge. Zionism as a warm, Jewish nationalism, a success? Of course Zionism could capture the hearts and minds of the already warm Galut Jew of Eastern Europe, the one whose Israeli grandson would later be ashamed of him. He whose Jewishness flowed from the ancient, traditional totality of Judaism quivered with excitement as the three-times-daily prayer, "And may our eyes behold thy return to Zion in mercy," teetered on the edge of reality. And it mattered little that he had wandered away from Judaism, for the faith had stamped its indelible impression on his nostalgic soul.

The Jew who had been warmed by the Sabbath candles, the Yemenite who had slept with Maimonides' epistle in the face of centuries of Muslim fanaticism, the countless Jews for whom the Galut was a daily affirmation of all of the Bible's dire predictions of disaster —all hungered for relief from the goy and his land. For such people, Zionism was a simple thing; they neither understood nor were concerned over the ramifications of a secular nationalism or Saul Tchernichowski's pagan yearnings or Ber Borochov's meanderings about a return to Zion so as to prepare for the class struggle or Jacob Klatzkin's obsession with "redeeming the basis of our being from spirituality." The Jew who had heard of the great Theodor Herzl, and who groaned in Lomzhe or Minsk or Sa'ana, thought of Zion as a place where he could continue to light his candles, say his Psalms, marry off his daughters to nice Jewish boys, or simply live like a man—all in a land that was miraculously free of the cursed goyim who made his life such a hell.

And of course, Zionism could deeply affect a certain number of enlightened Jews. Herzl and Leon Pinsker were born in the Exile and their illusions were shattered, their fondest dreams destroyed, their souls shaken to the core. They knew from their own personal experiences that there was no salvation among the gentiles, and Pinsker could gloomily declare to an advocate of assimilation: "I was also a visionary, an idealist, a member of that church which raised the ideals of equality and brotherhood to the highest level. . . . we hoped to be appreciated for our deeds, and what is our reward?"

And Herzl could watch cultured France go mad in an anti-Semitic Dreyfusian orgy and, shattered, write: "The fact of the matter is, everything tends to one and the same conclusion, which is expressed in the classic Berlin cry: *Juden raus!*" Certainly men like these who had tasted the bitter fruits of illusory freedom could be moved to a revulsion against the old dream of assimilation and an embracing of Zionism as an escape from the world they had experienced and knew to be a menace for the Jew. It is not strange that many such Jews should throw away the illusion of universalism and embrace total and exclusive Jewish nationalism. For although it was secular and although it was totally negative—merely fleeing from exile's pain—it was enough for the Jew faced with that pain.

But even among the secular Zionists, there were those who understood the intellectual dilemma of a Jewish nationalism that was no longer divinely special, but was merely an escape from persecution—a "no choice but." They could not simply accept a Jewish state that was forced upon them by the goy. They needed something more, something positive that *they* could direct, rather than have imposed upon them by circumstances and the outside world. And so we had an Ahad Ha-am who would resort to all manner of artificial contrivances to explain why Jews are "different" and "special" and "chosen" (a theory that, shorn of its divine elements, becomes narrowly foolish at best, and absurdly racist at worst), who created the concept of "natural nationalism," the survival of the Jews because of their "natural national will to survive"—and then never bothered to prove why their mystical urge was justified. Or Martin Buber, attempting to find a logical reason for the *affirmative* continuation of a separate Jewish people in the face of nondivine life, and ending up by sinking into a muddled mysticism of the "blood continuum of the people," an irrational, creative mystery uniting the generations, concepts that were sure to find adherents among those who assumed that precisely because they could not understand them, the theories must be deep and perceptive. Or the Socialists who added their own peculiar thinking (whether Borochovian or the more diluted Syrkinian) in order to give something more to a sterile and frustrating secular nationalism that—if the goy would have only allowed—they would have not needed and would have avoided on their direct route toward proletarian universalism.

But the sabra is none of these. He has not tasted the meaning of the Galut and not despaired of the goy, and so he is not driven by the fears and depression of Herzl. He does not remember the persecution and isolation of the Jew in the ghetto and the embracing of a warm Judaism that, alone, made him a meaningful and self-respecting figure. He is not a fiddler on the roof. He has no warm memories of a Jewish childhood and all the nostalgic guilt feelings that were engendered in those who are afraid to cast off all their Judaism. He has no need to invent positive but artificial reasons for Jewish nationalism and the Return to Zion, because he was born there. He has no need to add to his secular nationalism because it is as natural to him as being an Englishman or a Frenchman.

And precisely because of this, more and more Israelis begin to carry their secular "normal" nationalism to its logical conclusion. They divest it totally of any spark of specialness and move to a Jewishness that is more and more an Israeli-ness. For even secular Jewishness carries with it too much of an artificially contrived and abnormal nationalism. It implies one Jewish nation and a special and uncomfortably "racist" character about its Jewish members, most of whom live outside the sabra's land. What an abnormal and unnecessary problem! Being an Israeli, being normal, means divesting oneself of all this special Jewishness. For why be Jewish? This is the question, and unlike his Galut cousin (the relationship has been reduced to that degree) he is not plagued (and helped) by goyim who give him his answer by declaring: "Because we say you are" or by a minority status that makes him different from the sovereign majority about him. Why be Jewish if that means a nation that is extraterritorial, complex, anachronistic in its religious ethnocentricity; with a religion that is so odious and grating on one's freedom to be free; whose secular priests are always babbling about some *shtetl* in Poland that the "new" Jew never saw and could care less about; whose exclusiveness, codified in the Law of Return and in a Zionism of a Jewish majority state, is so patently chauvinistic, if not "racist"; whose exclusiveness contributes so much to Arab hostility. Ahavat Yisroel—love of Jewry—the concept that binds Jews all over the world into one warm and loving unit, that creates a Jewish people no matter where it exists, that is "the separation between Jewry and the nations" becomes at best anachronistic and at worst racist and dangerous the moment the Jew loses his religious raison d'être. And here is the heart of the problem.

The Chosen People: Questions 73

To many thousands of young sabras (some consciously and many others much more vaguely) there is a rejection of the Zionism of founding fathers who cherished an illusion. The illusion was that they could divest Jewishness of its divine origin, of its Sinaitic Revelation, of its religious chosenness, and still raise a new Jew who would be proud of his Jewishness, who would look upon all Jews as part of one people, and who would proudly retain his exclusiveness and separate identity. More than a few sabras react in amazement at such thoughts, for those who never have lived in Kasrilivka or would not have created it had they been there, are incapable of understanding what it is and what it implies.

Instead we see the sabra who finds it increasingly easy to "relate" to the Israeli Arab in his class at the university. We see the sabra who speaks of himself as an Israeli, not a Jew. We see the sabra who, finding life exceedingly difficult in the land that—aside from emotional nostalgia—is not particularly special in any way, goes off to Australia or Canada to make his fortune.

The Sabra is Klatzkin and Joseph Brenner in the sense that he has totally divested Jewishness of its special character and spirit, in that he can say with them that "we, the new Jews, have nothing to do with Judaism," and can speak with them as "the last Jews or the first Hebrews." But he is more than that. He is moving determinedly to the step that even those Zionist nihilists never took, the de-Zionization and de-Judaizing of himself, the "non-Arab" who lives in Israel. Not only is Jewishness now "cleansed" of Judaism, but for the descendant of the Jew who is now in the Land, the time has come to make a clean break with Jewishness as well. Because, at bottom, there is no reason to cleave to a chauvinistic nationalism that binds Jews together through an antiquated religious or national creed while setting up barriers of hostility between Israelis of different creeds—Jews and Arabs.

Not only is the Jewish religion rejected but also the Jewish nation, as not relevant to the new nationality—"Israeli" or "Hebrew" or "Canaanite." So while most have reached the point where they declare: "First I am Israeli, and only then a Jew," others have gone further and eliminated any order of priorities. It is only Israel that has national meaning and not Jewishness.

Let us be honest with ourselves and cease pointing to the prowess of Israeli youth in the army as proof of their loyal Jewishness. Certainly, there are many idealists, but for the vast majority it has nothing to do with Jewishness. It is the very normal, very universal reaction of a people faced with the threat of extermination. It is not their sense of Jewish historic destiny and peoplehood, but the knowledge that they will be thrown into the sea and that their personal lives and fortunes are at stake, that drives them to conquer mountains. It is the defense of country that motivates, not the concept of Jewish people and historical destiny.

And let us note here something of major importance. The majority of Israelis who proclaim a desire to return at least a portion of the lands liberated in 1967 are motivated by honest, though ill-advised, motives of peace. But there are others in this camp, mostly younger Israelis, who are different.

The Chosen People: Questions

For more and more of these young Israelis to ask: "Why should we not return the lands or why should Arabs not be allowed to return?" is not merely compromise for the sake of peace. It represents loss of understanding and rejection of this land as the Jewish Land of Israel in its entirety. This philosophical point of departure stems from the feeling that the time has come to compromise the "chauvinistic" feeling of exclusiveness of *land* because the time has also come to reject the "racist" concept of exclusiveness of *people*. The attitude of this kind of young Israeli to the land is not only one of pragmatic compromise but one of *ideology*. He is prepared to share his land with Arabs because he sees no great reason for not sharing with the Arabs his peoplehood. The concept of a Chosen Land has become irrelevant and meaningless to many an Israeli and this is only a barometer of his feelings about a Chosen People.

It is not enough for the frustrated, elderly Zionist Fathers of the Nation to complain about the lessening of Zionism and Jewish identity among the young Israelis. Golda Meir's exhortation to American Jews to teach their children Hebrew so that they will not lose their Jewishness echoes hollowly among thousands of Hebrew-speaking sabras who couldn't care less about their Jewishness (including many who are actively working to de-Zionize Mrs. Meir's Jewish State and on behalf of the oppressed "Palestinians"). Ben Gurion's glorifying of the ancient Israelite, Joshua, brings only bored yawns from most students and angry comments from others about the barbaric practices of the conqueror of Canaan. Secular Jewish nationalism, like all the modern Jewish streams that attempted to dilute Judaism of its exclusive, revealed divine character, ends up in an intellectual and very real dead end for the confused Jew of our day.

Again, at bottom, what plagues the young Jews (and many more adults who care to so admit publicly) both in the Galut and in Israel, who have lost their sense of divine election and uniqueness, is the simple question: Why be a Jew? And the one responds by becoming an American while the other turns into an Israeli, with increasing numbers of both declaring: Let us rather be human beings.

For Israel, the practical consequences of such thinking are clear: Increasing indifference to Jewish problems outside of Israel along with growing hostility to Jewish immigration from the Galut; the striking down of all social barriers to intercourse with the Arabs and increasing intermarriage and assimilation (particularly on the part of the many Sephardic and "progressive" Jewish girls who showed similar modernism by leaping into black beds in the United States); demands that Arab fears of Jewish "expansion" be met by amending—or abolishing—the Law of Return; marching, demonstrating, and violently protesting on behalf of the "oppressed" Israeli Arabs who are second-class citizens, and turning the country into a replica of so many other western countries where restless and nonidentifying youth sought victims of oppression they could "defend" with all the resultant anarchy and upheaval; demanding recognition of the "Palestinian" nation and state at the price of Jewish land and Jewish security; increasing calls for de-Zionization of Israel and its evolution into a non-sectarian Middle East state; escalating emigration to western countries where there are no Arab threats of extermination and much more money to be made (for why stay in an Israel with more problems than other countries when it is no different from other countries?); decreasing immigration from advanced, western countries (for why give up the materially good life to come to a country that is the same, only poorer?); more and more alienation from any kind of religious practice with tentative efforts to introduce the dishonest quasi-Judaism of the West, and the introduction of civil marriage and divorce that will irrevocably split the nation into two separate camps; a disastrous rise in violence and crime as religious sanction disappears; escalation of non-Jewish moral and cultural values that destroy the discipline and sacrifice of Jewishness and Zionism; increasing materialism, with envy and jealousy of "haves" on the part of "have nots" that can lead to a socio-economic war of brothers and a corresponding lack of social justice and compulsion on the part of the greedy rich.

Those who must be squarely blamed for the creation of a youth with ever-lessening Jewish identity and who will force Israel into political moves that will endanger her very existence, are the ones who have allowed the school curriculum, the communications media, and the general national atmosphere to reflect a bland (at best), and even a negative attitude toward proud, specific Jewish nationalism. The schools of Israel do not aim at creating warm, proud, deeply nationalistic views. They are *western*, not Jewish schools. They aim

OUR CHALLENGE 78

at putting out an educated and professional man, not a deeply knowledgeable and intense Jew. They are massive failures in *Jewish* education and we will pay a terrible price for their failures.

Not only is the Jewish youngster not exposed to much-needed long and intense hours of nationalist indoctrination, so that his knowledge of the Jewish freedom fighters of our times—the Irgun, Lechi (Sternists) and Haganah in Israel and the partisan fighters in the Exile—is weak and shallow, thus creating the impression of an "imperialist," nonrevolutionary state. Not only is no total effort made to teach him about the present life of the Jew, his brother, in the Galut so as to tie the two together with deep and intense bonds. Not only is the intense hatred for the Jew by the gentile not deeply impressed on the young Jew's brow along with the universal lesson that Jew-hatred is a *halakha l dorot* (an eternal law), thus saving us future adventures in Jewish illusions.

There is a greater failure, the failure to understand that unless the young Jewish child in Israel is deeply impressed with the exclusiveness of the Jewish people and the divine election of Israel he will see no reason to be Jewish religiously or nationally and no reason to have a Zionist, Jewish state that leads only to war and tension. He will see no reason to perpetuate a Zionist and Jewish-majority consciousness that is "logically" racist and chauvinist. He will see no great reason for close and warm ties with Jews overseas. He will see no reason to oppose intermarriage and assimilation and to set up barriers between Jew and Arab. What I am saying is that we run the risk of having large numbers of our youth take the ultimate step: from throwing off religion, to casting away *Jewish* nationalism for "Israeli-iness," to opposition to an *Israeli* state that creates barriers to peace with the Arabs.

Unless the Jew is special, chosen, and different we will continue to have results such as those revealed in the careful and brilliant study made of the attitudes of Israeli high school children by Professor Simon Herman.

That survey showed a shocking lack of interest in and a deep negativism concerning Jewish values. Thus, in response to the question, "Does the fact that you are Jewish play an important part in your life?" some 25 percent replied that it was of little importance, while no fewer than 7 percent said none.

"If you were to be born again would you wish to be born a Jew?" brought a response by fully 28 percent that it was a matter of indifference to them, with 2 percent flatly admitting that they would not. When the same question was posed as, "If you were to live outside of Israel, would you wish to be born a Jew?" a staggering 21 percent said no, with 25 percent saying it made no difference to them. The negativists become a majority when one eliminates the many Orthodox students who took part in the survey –all of whom responded affirmatively. One need hardly add that on the question of personal intermarriage 27 percent declared that they would marry a non-Jew if the occasion arose. It is important to quote Professor Herman's gloomy conclusion:

"Significant differences consistently appear on Jewish-identity items between religious, traditionalist, and nonreligious students. The Jewish identity of the religious student is much stronger than that of the traditionalist and nonreligious student; the Jewish identity of the traditionalist is stronger than that of the nonreligious student. . . . Not only do the religious students feel more Jewish and value their Jewishness more under all circumstances, but they feel closer to, and have a greater identification with, Jews everywhere." Bear in mind that this survey was taken in 1964; since then the identity problem has grown significantly worse.

It may be most unpleasant for some but at least honest to recognize that unless *Judaism* is brought into the schools (and by this I do not mean the bland Bible class that is taught by disbelievers as an exercise in futile hypocrisy), then *Jewishness* will also begin to disappear. Unless an immediate effort is made to introduce into the schools religious subjects taught by trained religious teachers with the point of emphasizing that element of the Jewish people that makes them different, there will be no point to being different.

The Ministry of Education knows this and understands exactly what should be done, but it fears to act because it fears the possible creation of a generation of religious youngsters who will weaken the power of the Labor Establishment and its hold on the government. And the Israeli Establishment, devoted as it is to the people and state, is more devoted to the perpetuation of its own power.

Jewish nationalism cannot long exist in a meaningful way without the Jewish religion, and the Jewish religion remains vapid and empty without Revelation and Jewish election as a Chosen People. These concepts must be introduced into the schools, and the Jewish books and sources from which we derive these concepts must be studied and absorbed by our little children before we lose them.

We must learn from the disaster of the past hundred and fifty years and return to the sources from which our fathers derived their pride in self and the strength to survive, to overcome, to return to the Land. We must relearn and teach those basic concepts that always were the mainstream of historical Jewry and that every Jew, to his delight and salvation, once believed in. Above all, the disaster that is education in Israel must be totally overhauled and reshaped along the proud lines of Jewish nationalism and tradition. The truth of Jewish tradition and Torah values must be reintroduced to the grandchildren of a people that once believed and observed it.

It is not merely a question of making the young Jew religious, although that is surely the ideal. More important is the fact that without a basic knowledge of Judaism and heritage it becomes ultimately impossible to create a people totally committed to itself and its destiny. It is no longer possible, especially with sensitive and introspective Jewish youth, to create a proud and committed nation on the basis of nationalism alone. Pure nationalism no longer suffices to claim the loyalties and souls of youth. It is illogical and chauvinistic for them to hear demands for absolute loyalty based on the artificial divisions of people and boundaries. There must be something unique and different that calls for their loyalty or they will not give it.

And there must be something that binds the youth into a disciplined and sacrificing being, or else he will descend into the same maelstrom of violence, crime, class struggle, selfish demanding, and materialistic grubbing that destroy all other societies. Nationalism and patriotism have long since failed in this respect.

It is only the uniqueness of the divine seal that gives the young Jew the difference, the *ha-mavdil beyn yisroel l'amim,* the separation of Israel from the nations. It is this that calls him to be different, to stamp Jewishness on himself and his state. It is only this that helps him to understand the meaning of Jewish suffering throughout the ages and the stubborn defiance, on the part of his forefathers, of the world that demanded that the Jew assimilate and disappear. Unless the young Jew begins to understand something of the true and deep values of Judaism he will never be able to understand why Jews suffered for the Sabbath, for kashrut, against intermarriage. He will never be able to comprehend a Mattathias and his Maccabean sons rising up and risking all for laws that appear so antiquated and that his society mocks. For the one who questions his history has no future since he who does not understand where he came from cannot know where he is going.

It is, therefore, not enough that the young Jew should be observant. There is more to it than that. If not for himself, at least let him understand the depth and greatness of Judaism and the need to have the character and color of the nation and state stamped with Jewish uniqueness. At least let him understand that the nation and state are special things. Only then will he give them both his pure and unadulterated self.

How can this be done? In only one way.

Jewish education. The Jewish school in Israel. This is where Judaism and Jewish nationalism begin their progress into the heart and mind of the Jewish youngster. This is where a successful Jew is molded—or a disastrous one. Today the schools of Israel turn out a series of unmitigated Jewish disasters. We have created schools whose model is the western school, which strives at turning out the model of the western man. They are schools which succeed in producing good doctors, lawyers, architects, scientists. And so they are disasters. For they fail utterly in producing a warm, proud, nationalist Jew. And the worst of it is that they do not try! This is not the aim of the school curriculum, this is not the target that the Ministry of Education sets its eyes upon. There is no real Jewish education in the schools of Israel. We see the bitter results today, and we shall pay a mighty and bitter price tomorrow.

A school is a place to indoctrinate, to mold and to shape young minds and souls. Those who do not think so contribute to our disaster. Nonvalue schools produce nonvalue children. Western-type schools produce western-type children. Jewish schools, whose avowed aim is to produce proud, knowledgeable, unique Jews, do just that. Only they do that.

A parent has a duty to indoctrinate the child. His or her obligation is to instill in the child the values of the parent. The parent who fails to do this is a failure as a parent. The same is true of a state. The schools it creates must reflect the values of the state and the people, and ours do not. Our children do not emerge with pride in themselves as a unique and special people. They are not overwhelmed with the magnificence and the truth of their tradition. They do not glow with soulful pride in their history and the achievements of their fathers. They do not look back with pride on the sacrifices and dedication of their ancestors in the Exile or the flaming actions of those who returned to till the soil and smash the British imperialist enemy. They emerge like all other children anywhere in the western world, with the same shallow values, the same vapid, materialistic dreams, the same boredom and feeling that life is empty and boring. These are your gods, O schools of Israel.

The schools must be changed or we are doomed as a people and state. The entire curriculum must be changed, the entire approach and direction must be changed.

Today the overwhelming majority of our children rush into the streets whose shining lights speak of discotheques, automobiles, girls (and boys), money (hopefully) in one's pocket, good times, excitement, the lure of New York or Paris or London. They envy life American-style, little appreciating its moral, spiritual, and existential bankruptcy. No matter, they worship it; they adore it; they hang on to every English word on television, every irrational song and beat, every mad style and mode. The Land of Israel is less than special for them; it is a land that is poor and where work is demanding and pay is low. Elsewhere the lights glitter and good times beckon. And they yearn to get out.

There are really no such things as no-value schools. For if schools do not teach values, the vacuum that is the child's soul is filled with values picked up in the streets. The materialism that corrodes the soul demands fulfillment, and so crime and prostitution become ways to achieve the good life that the products of Israeli education yearns for. Violence and sadism and brutality and utter lack of concern for anyone else ease the frustrations of those who cannot achieve the bright lights and glitter that is all that matters to them in life. And should there come, G-d forbid, an economic recession, then we will watch while all those who are so lacking in elementary discipline and concern for the good of the state, even in good times, turn into protesting, demonstrating, even violent demanders of "more." All the social problems and communal problems and class struggles will emerge in all their fury—and where will *ahavat Yisroel* be, to moderate and block the war between brothers? It will not be there. For the same schools that did not teach the uniqueness of the Jew, *could not* teach the need to place Jewish national and brotherly values first.

For a minority, more sensitive and intelligent, the nonvalue vacuum is filled by questioning and searching for ideals. Is it surprising that there are those who question the basic values and sacred cows of Israel? Wait, we have seen only the beginning. We have only begun to drink from the bitter potion that we ourselves have stirred.

Overhaul the schools, I say. Make them places of Jewish indoctrination, instilling Jewish values from the youngest age. From the time the Jew enters his school at kindergarten, let the aim be to instill in him the knowledge and belief that the Jewish people and tradition are divinely chosen, unique and true. Let the knowledge of his glorious history, taught in a prideful way, flow over him. Let him open a traditional Jewish book and, under the guidance of sympathetic, believing teachers, let him begin to understand the warmth and beauty of its substance and why, for these books like these, his great-grandparents were prepared to make the ultimate sacrifice.

Let the pride of the Revolt, of the Irgun and Lechi and Palmach and Haganah fill his mind at an early age. Let him know of the heroes of the nation who went to the gallows and let him mark their passing with bowed head and their exploits with joy. What normal nation hides its heroes from its youth? Only the abnormal one that is in the hands of politicians.

Let Zionism be taught and Zionist history—in detail and with positive pride. Let the story of the Jewish communities in the Galut be taught so that the ties between Jews here and there are strengthened. Let the names of Jewish heroes throughout the ages be learned and known in depth, and not superficially. Let the Holocaust be a meaningful thing for the young Israeli from earliest childhood and let it be taught with pride in that which once was sadness for that which disappeared. Let the exploits of Jewish partisans and freedom fighters of Eastern Europe be known. In short, let Jewish nationalism infuse the mind and the spirit of the Jewish youngster in Eretz Yisroel from the day that he enters the Jewish school.

Yet, let us remember that while it is vital to begin immediately to strengthen, reinforce, and add to the nationalist indoctrination of our young children, to overhaul the sterility and empty national education of our schools, in the end it is not in mere secular nationalism, like that of other nations, that we will find the real answer to the salvation of our national soul and the redemption of our confused children. It is not secular education and not secular movements or parties that hold the key. For while energetic nationalist education will halt the tide temporarily and save not a few from the purposelessness of their lives, the secular nationalist can never succeed in giving an honest answer to the question: Why be a Jew? And if there is one thing that youth both in Israel and outside demands, it is honesty.

Israelis used to maintain (and many of the less perceptive still do) that assimilation was impossible in Israel and that, therefore, religion and Judaism were not necessary for the existence of the people. Aside from the patently false assumption that the spiritual characteristic of the Jew was simply an artificial attempt to save him from disappearing and served no other function; aside from the obvious question of what in the world is so important about saving a people from assimilating if there is nothing special about that people; aside from this—the fact is that the statement is false in itself. The Jew in Israel *can* assimilate in the sense that he slowly changes from a Jew into an "Israeli," dropping everything that made him unique and weakening all the ties that bind him to the Jew outside of the Land. He can assimilate because he sees no good reason for remaining a Jew and a great many reasons for not. The thought that by rejecting Jewishness he also abandons every moral right to the Land of the Jewish people (for, after all, what except the *Jewish* claim allowed his fathers to enter a land inhabited by Arabs for hundreds of years) does not concern him. He rejects the specialness of the Jew because he correctly perceives that without the divine faith of the Jew there *is* no specialness. He becomes a normal Israeli. He assimilates into the Middle East and the world and tries to do what every assimilationist in the Galut tried to do.

He suffers from schizophrenia, this young Israeli, and he seeks to escape it. The disease is foisted on him by all those Zionist founding fathers who insist that he remain true to his Jewish people and his Jewish state and then proceed to divest their own lives and their own Jewishness of anything special. Older people may understand the dilemmas and frauds of their lives but are too weary and too frightened to own up to them. Younger ones find it much simpler to be honest wreckers, and we see them at work today.

Noar Zahav. It is true: they are gold, and they are good and they can be fine Jews and they want to be. It is not their fault if their homes, their schools, and their state leave them hungry and yearning for uniquely Jewish answers. Again, I say, it is not only a question of young Jews who will observe Torah and *mitzvot*—although how wonderful it would be for them and for us if they did. But it is more than that. If not practicing, individual Jews, at least they should understand that the nation and state must be shaped and run along uniquely Jewish lines, that the personality and character of the people and state must reflect its Jewish heritage—at least that.

The struggle for the souls and minds of our youth is the greatest problem facing the State of Israel today. Before it, all other problems fade into insignificance, for their solutions depend largely on whether our Jewish youth will be proud Jews, good Jews, sacrificing Jews, Jews who conceive of themselves as uniquely different, hence bound together in one common ideal. Without this, he will see the constant wars with the Arabs and scream in frustration: who needs a new state if there is no end to the wars? He will either leave the country or turn his back on Zionism and the great dream for him will have the taste of ashes.

We ignore the problem or belittle it or underestimate it at our own peril. The jackals, the demagogues, the wreckers are already at work and we must meet them and give our youth the Idea. We must give them a reason for being Jews, a reason for holding on to the traditional and ancient Jewish values. We must define our youth; we must tell them who they are. We must answer their questions: What and why is a Jew? What and why am I?

4

The Chosen People: Definitions

"Now—Herefore, if ye will obey my voice indeed, and keep my covenant, then ye shall be a peculiar treasure unto me above all people; for all the earth is mine. And ye shall be unto me a kingdom of priests, and a holy nation..." (Exodus 19: 5-6). "Happy are we, how good is our portion, how pleasant our lot, how beautiful our inheritance" (from the morning prayer service).

More than three millennia ago, on a day like any other day, but incomparably more so, the world stood still for a brief moment in history. It was the moment for which history itself had been created. It was the moment in which the Jewish people came into being.

For the Jew of history, for all the generations of Jews beginning at that awesome moment at Sinai when the heavens shook and the earth trembled and an entire people heard the voice of its creator and saw the manifestations of his being and until our so very recent Age of Confusion, there was never a problem of identity. The Jewish people knew exactly what it was. It knew when it came into being, why it came into being, what was expected of it, and what its ultimate destiny would be.

The Jew who was our ancestor—down to our great-grandfathers and grandfathers—knew that the Jewish nation was a nation like no other. This was not merely another Moab or Canaan or Edom or Persia or Greece or Albania or Bulgaria. There is precious little need in the world for one more obnoxious nation-state. This nation had not come into being through the usual evolution of a handful of tribes into a permanent, larger entity. The Jewish nation had a specific moment it could point to when it became a nation. The Jew could lay his finger upon that moment in history and say: Here is *where* and here is *when* I became a people. It was at the moment of Sinai, with the entire nation standing in a sublime instant of awe and incomprehensible joy, that the L-rd revealed himself and created his nation.

And the Jew always knew that there was a *reason* for this new nation's being. He knew that an everlasting covenant had been agreed to on that day. *"V'atem tihiyu li mamlechet kohanim v'goy kadosh"* ("And you shall be for me a priestly kingdom and a holy nation") was dependent upon *"im shamoa tishmiy b'koli ushmartem et briti"* ("if you shall hearken unto my voice and safeguard my covenant"). Only for the Jew did the world come into being and only because of the Torah was the Jew created.

The Torah, the word of G-d, the perfect Law even when imperfect man cannot fathom all its depths. The Torah, the way of life that leads to *kedusha* and perfection. And Torah, the condition for Jewish nationhood whose relationship with its Jews determines Jewish future and destiny. All that would befall the Jew, for good or bad, was predicated on his relationship to the Law. It was a destiny that was irrevocable and the Jew, try as he might, could not and would not ever escape from it. This was his election; this was why he was chosen. Not as a "master race." Not as a "superior race." But chosen for Torah, commandments, and holiness.

And the Jew knew that he, the Chosen People of the chosen Law, had been given a chosen Land. And that land was his, for from the moment that G-d, the creator and possessor of heaven and earth, decreed that this land was Israel's, irrevocable title was issued in the name of the Jew. All past claims and all future claims became irrelevant. The Land was the Land of Israel and no one else's. Here the Jew was to fullfill his destiny, to reach his potential, to achieve *kedusha* (holiness). Only here was *kedusha* and everything else outside the boundaries of the Holy Land was *tumah,* impurity, and

Galut, exile. The land of Israel represented spiritual and physical safety and *chutz l'aretz* (outside the Land) symbolized physical and spiritual danger.

Little wonder that such a people was trained to ignore the pettiness of life, to reject the vanities and the transitory foolishness that crossed its path. Great people have no time for petty ventures and the Jewish people was created for greatness. Little wonder that the persecutions and sufferings that befell the Jew were looked upon with the proper perspective of temporariness that they deserved. This was an eternal people and eternal men do not bother with the momentary distresses of history. Neither persecution nor derision can move a man who knows that he is correct, who has pride in himself and his life, who likes himself and respects himself, who is blessed with the truth that leads to *hadar,* pride.

It is time that we and our children knew of Jewish greatness and Jewish destiny. It is time that we gave ourselves a Jewish reason for being. It is time for *hadar.*

Hadar! That noble giant of our times, Zev Jabotinsky, touched upon the pride of the Jew, the nobility and grandeur that follow him throughout the generations, when he wrote:

Hadar! A Jew, even in poverty, is
a nobleman;
Whether slave or serf you were
created a Prince,
Crowned with the diadem of David . . .

What is *hadar?* If he would truly know Jewish pride, if he would truly feel the confidence of self-respect and dignity, the Jew must go back and return to an understanding of what it is that makes a Jew different. Judaism —heritage, tradition, philosophy—from this comes the very essence of *hadar*.

As I once wrote: "Our grandfather stood upon a burning mountain and conversed with G-d. He brought back with him a gift called the Torah. The world was never the same since." Jewish pride begins with the knowledge that it was we who gave the world the concept of the one, merciful G-d who created man so that he might reach holiness. This was the beginning of that civilization man has so unceasingly reached for until this very day.

Our pride lies in the concept, "Hear O Israel, the L-rd is our G-d, the L-rd is One." In the fact that G-d lifted us from mediocrity and proclaimed for us a difficult but magnificent task: "And thou shalt be for me a special people, a kingdom of priests and a holy nation." Up from mediocrity, up to holiness—this is the hallmark of the Jew.

Those who wrap themselves in the Marxist prayer shawl and thrice daily bless the Jew-hating economist for having given the world social justice and conscience, incredibly ignore the justice and liberty that was proclaimed by Judaism, its prophets and rabbis, long before there was a Lenin or a Mao. Thus spoke our rabbis in the Talmud:

Just as the Almighty is called merciful and gracious, thou too, be merciful and gracious. Just as the Almighty is called righteous, thou too, be righteous. Just as he is abundant in goodness, thou too, be abundant in goodness. Just as the Almighty is called Holy, thou too, be holy.

The call to holiness is the seal of the Jew and the way to achieve that holiness—that rising above base, selfish, animal limitation to a world of spirit, giving, and sacrifice—is achieved only through the unqiue Jewish way of life, the observance of the *mitzvot,* the commandments, of the Torah.

In profound realization that the evil of man's actions stems from his weakness and that only a stong and mature man can overcome that weakness and temptation that urges him on to commit evil, the Torah lays down a daily and, indeed, minute-by-minute regimen and a disciplined way of life to create within the Jew the habit of giving, of doing without, of sacrificing, so that he learns the true values of life and how to rise to the demands and obstacles that threaten those values.

It is not evil but weakness, not criminality but immaturity that are at the heart of man's failure to reach holiness. It is to create a mature and spiritually strong Jew that the Torah sets as its task.

What a tragedy that the Jew is so abysmally ignorant of himself and his own treasures: How pitful that he has not the slightest knowledge of the diamonds that he threw away when he rejected Judaism for bagels and lox, Miami Beach, and the Conservative and Reform Temple charades! What irony that that which the young Jew searches for belonged to his grandfather and that the son of the latter destroyed his own offspring by denying to his own child the heritage that he himself perverted!

Who will tell the young Jew, who races about frantically seeking himself, that *kashrut* is not an outdated thing which originally came into being because the clever Jews of yore knew what was clean while the stupid goyim ate dirt? Who will see in it the discipline that demands the ability to give up a food that one might be hungry for, in order to dampen that basic yearning of man for food and thus bring him a little closer to the angels and raise him a little higher than the beast of the field?

And who will tell the young Jew that his father— and Reform rabbi—are both ignoramuses when they delight in telling us that the Sabbath comes to stop us from "work" and thus modern man has no longer any need for the Mosaic antiquity? Who will show him the beauty of a day that forbids not work but production of any kind, laborious or done with flick of a switch, in order that man for at least one day of the week may divest himself of his hunger for profits and his illusion that he is the creator and determiner of the progress of the world.

Society and the world will never change until man does, and goodness and mercy will not settle on the general world until the particular man within it is good and merciful. And that man will not and cannot change without a demanding and disciplined way of life that turns him from a child into an adult, from a weak and demanding creature into a mature and sacrificing one.

And so, Judaism imposes upon man the *mitzvot,* the commandments that are the yoke that sets him free. No, not a paradox, for it is the "liberated" man and woman, free to do whatever they please, who are, in truth, enslaved. They are prisoners to their own desires, frustrations, searchings, bodies. It is only the man who can tell his body and his impulse, "no!" who is truly a man free and emancipated.

Jewish tradition and heritage! A return to the source of Jewish uniqueness so that we may understand the essence of *hadar* and so that we may know the power of pride and self-respect. Is there any wonder that our people smiled with that power of *hadar* even as they were degraded and ground into the dust? One cannot degrade those who are called the children of the Almighty. One cannot grind into the dust those who are but a little lower than the angels. One who knows where he came from and where he is going is free of all fear of contempt by others and its most dangerous result—self-hatred.

The Jewish people looks forward to the day when "The L-rd shall be king over all the earth: on that day will the L-rd be one and his name one." It is then, in the end of days, that "All mankind will call in your name ... and they shall accept your sovereignty." This dream of universal brotherhood, based on the acceptance of the truth of the kingdom of the L-rd and his Law, is the ultimate Jewish one. But to speak of a universality not based on the divine truth of Torah is to speak of both falsehood and illusion. Mere unity of peoples has never created a better society—witness the Communist delusion. Mere integration and knocking down of barriers assures us of nothing better than before. Indeed, one unified world based on falsehood, corruption, and evil is infinitely the worst of all things, for then, man has no place on this earth to which to flee and to practice truth and goodness. Universality, yes. But only under an idea that truly transforms Man into a better being. This idea, for the Jew, is Torah, and until that idea is accepted there can be no assimilation, integration, and elimination of barriers between Jew and gentile. Such a falsely assimilated world will see the uniqueness of Jewish identity eliminated and, with it, all hope of changing the world.

Separation of the Jew from the non-Jewish world always meant separation and preservation of the Jewish idea from contamination and assimilation. If it is true that *"Ata Bchartanu mikal ha'amim"* ("Thou hast chosen us from all the nations") then it is also true that the same "thou" is also the one who is *"hamavdil beyn kodesh l'chol . . . beyn Yisroel l'amim"* ("separates the holy from the profane . . . Israel from the nations"). The Jewish demand for separation is based on the axiom that truth and falsehood cannot mix lest the truth become impaired and eventually threatened with extinction. The Jew can love mankind but he need not go to bed with it. Judaism can teach its truths to man but only when it stands aside, separated and chosen. If we have pride in the perfection of Torah we would be worse than mad to destroy it by assimilation and integration. Jewish *hadar* speaks of the uniqueness of the Jew, of the perfection of his Torah and of the need to preserve this *havdala*—separatism.

Hadar is achieved too through a study of Jewish history, that magnificent chronicle of a people which defies all logic. A deep, intensive, and faithful study of this history is absolutely necessary for the children of our age.

Our age. If we seek a proper label for our times, if we search for some phrase to describe this era in which we live, we could find none better then the Age of Confusion.

How lost we are and how broken are the compasses that we so frantically snatch! How awesome is our fear of freedom, the freedom we demanded so loudly. How unsure and how lost we are and how pitifully we fall deeper and deeper into the quicksand as we thrash about desperately searching for the firm land of stability. And how much nonsense does this confusion engender and how much self-hate and how much self-destruction!

And those who suffer most, who are the most confused, are our youth. How little our youth know about themselves and how much they begin to despise themselves and those who made them what they are. How absent the self-respect; how lacking the *hadar*. How much they need, these youngsters, who question the specialness of the Jew and his claim to his Land, to peer into the history of their people and drink from that history the refreshing waters of pride. How important is this history for the sabra who increasingly speaks of "Palestine" and Jewish "intransigence" and the "brotherhood of nations" and the "de-Zionization of Israel."

Jewish history! That whirlpool of tragedy, drama, and courage, whose richness and color dazzle anyone who plunges into its depths. For the Jew whose ignorance of self is devastating, it is essential that he travel backward through the pages of his own times. It is necessary that he learn what his stubborn ancestors did or refused to do, and how, but for their obstinacy, he would not exist today.

How important it is for our youth to learn and to feel—as much as possible—the greatness and magnificence of the moment of return and all the events that led up to it. How important it is for us to teach them.

They must know about that moment on the fifth day of Iyar, as they stood in the streets. They, the Jews, the "Zionists," our people. The year that was 1948 to the world but which to us was 1878—one thousand eight hundred and seventy years since the beginning of the long Exile. For that is how Jews always counted their history.

We must never let them forget the moment, as the farmers, tailors, housewives, mechanics, students — and Auschwitz survivors—stood quietly, listening. Listening to a proclamation that marked an end and a beginning of an impossible dream come true. The words entered their ears, filled their minds, and flooded their eyes and hearts:

We hereby proclaim the establishment of the Jewish State in Palestine to be called Medinat Yisroel. . . .

And who can forget the moment when, as the words drifted off into the cloudless sky, the Jews of Tel-Aviv burst into song—*the* song:

Od lo avda tikvateynu . . .
Our hope is not yet lost,
The hope of two thousand years,
To be a free people in our land
The land of Zion and Jerusalem.

How they sang and how, for just that moment in time, they rose to the heights of immortality with tears streaming down their faces and joy beyond that of this world gripping their souls. Those Jews were witness to a fulfillment, an impossible fulfillment of an impossible journey and promise. In a word, they stood before a miracle: "And the people saw the L-rd . . . ."

It was the culmination of an odyssey that puts the most imaginative fiction to shame. It was the success of the Jew who had cried out to his G-d: "I shall not die but I shall live and tell of the creations of the L-rd". Of the Jew whose obstinacy and stubborness had worn down even his G-d.

Shall we not sit with tears of pride and remember how the Roman legions came and burned our Temple and drove us out of our land, but not before we fought like lions for every inch and enshrined the names of Bethar and Masada in the annals of bravery forever?

And shall we not, in amazement and disbelief, read the roll call of the enemies who vainly sought to erase the Jewish name from the face of the earth and who, themselves, are today but relics of the ancient past? Pharaoh, Assyria, Babylonia, Haman of Persia, Antiochus of the Greeks, Hadrian of the Romans, Christian fanatics throughout Europe and Asia Minor, Muslim fanatics in North Africa and the Middle East, and, in our own time, Nazi Germany and the Soviet Union.

Pharaoh drowned our babies and we survived him. The Amalekites demanded that we perish in the desert and we still live. Babylon exiled us and we returned. Haman plotted to wipe us out in one day and it was he who was hanged. Antiochus decreed that the Torah not be allowed to exist and today Jewish scholars tour the rotting monuments to a dead Greece. Titus built an arch to immortalize our demise and cried out, *"Judea capta,"* but Roman legions have long since vanished from the face of the earth.

When the Jew was scattered to the four corners of the earth he took with him his prayers and his belief that someday he would return home. The Byzantines could oppress him, the Chruch curse and shame him, the Inquisition, the Crusaders, and the feudal Christians seek his soul and take his body. The Muslims could steal his children in Yemen, drive him out of Granada, and enclose him in the ghettos of North Africa. He could be exiled from nation to nation, burned at the stake, be torn apart by drunken peasants in Poland and fanatic Arabs in the Orient, but the Jew, obsessed with his faith and the knowledge that he would survive, opened his Torah, believed in his G-d, and dreamed of Return. He would sit on the cold stone floor with flickering candles at his feet in countless synagogues on Tisha b'Av, the Day of Lamentations, and remember "the city that was filled with people hath become a widow." He would be beaten and pray, "Unto Jerusalem your city, return in mercy"; he would be burned and shout forth, "Next year in Jerusalem"; he would be gassed and say, "I believe with perfect faith that my eyes will behold your return in mercy to Zion."

Our grandfather who rose from the ruins of the burned Temple was the first Zionist. Herzl and Pinsker and Hess? It was not they who brought us back or who created Zionism. They were merely men whose time had come and who put into practice the dream that had been saved for them by the Jews of eternity. It was the stubborn and obstinate Jews, our fathers, who preserved Israel, which never had to come into being because it had never gone out of existence, in the mind and heart of the Jew. We owe no thanks to an Arthur Balfour or a League of Nations or a United Nations. Israel would have risen without them simply because the stubborness of a Jewish grandfather can be denied only so long.

Let us teach it unto our children and unto theirs, this magnificent chronicle of our people, for one who walks the footpaths of Jewish history can never be a self-hater, can never doubt the existence of his G-d. Within the story of the Jewish past we find ourselves, our pride, our belief, and our future.

There are too many among us who worship daily at the shrine of every "national liberation movement" in the world. They prostrate themselves before the feet of every Trotsky, Che, and Mao; every brown revolutionary is their god. They find revolt against oppression everywhere except among their own people. Heroes galore, except among Jews. "There are no Jewish heroes of the struggle against imperialism and there is no Jewish liberation," they cry.

How much we need to penetrate the minds and hearts of our youth and tell them the story of Jewish national liberation and revolt against the tyrant and the oppressor.

These are the things that we must teach our children day and night:

Of the mad Jewish students and ideologists who returned to their malaria-ridden desert of a land and, in the face of astonishment and ridicule, began to pluck it from its ruins.

Of the mad Jews named Jabotinsky and Trumpeldor who awoke one morning with the dream of a Jewish army—the first in two thousand years—and created a Jewish Legion whose ranks were filled with the motley and wonderfully strange people from Poland and Russia and London's East End.

Of Trumpeldor going down before the bullets of the "oppressed" Arabs with the words: "*Ayn davar . . . tov lamut ba'ad artzeynu*" (It doesn't matter . . . it's good to die for our country"). Had they been said by Che, every leftist in Israel would tatoo it on his breast.

Of the years 1920, 1921, 1929, 1936-39, the years of Arab riots against women, children and religious students.

Of Perfidious Albion's cynical efforts to destroy the dream of a Jewish state by cutting off the east bank of Eretz Yisroel and creating a puppet farce called "Transjordan." Of the further efforts by the imperialist British to side with the Arabs by looking away from every "revolutionary" riot and rape and by limiting all Jewish colonization and immigration.

Of the rise of Jewish heroes who proclaimed that Jewish blood is not *hefker,* cheap and for the taking, and that it is not a *mitzva* to die like a dog at the hands of the goy. Of the burial of the madness known as *havlaga,* self-restraint, and the striking back with Jewish fist and bullet. Of the creation of the magnificent Irgun Zvai Leumi and Fighters for the Freedom of Israel who showed the non-Jew that the "old Jew" of the Land of Israel and been resurrected and who taught his more timid brothers the lesson that Esau respects only strength.

Of the name Shlomo Ben Yosef, the first Jew to go to the gallows under the tyrant British, who served as the example for Jewish courage and revolt for all those who would follow, shouting: *"Lamut o lichbosh et hahar"* (To die or to conquer the mount").

Of David Raziel who fell fighting the Nazis in Iraq while the Arab revolutionaries there were backing Hitler (as had the leader of the Arab "freedom fighters," the Mufti, and Anwar Sadat). Of Hannah Senesh, who dropped into Nazi-occupied Hungary to try to save her brothers destined for slaughter, and who was shot by the Nazis.

Of Yair, Avraham Stern, who wrote of the nameless men who build a state with blood and fire.

Of the *Struma* and *Patria* and all the ships with desperate refugees that did not manage to get through and of all the Jews who never even managed to get aboard a ship to be turned back. Of all the ships that did get through because the Haganah persisted in defying the oppressor.

Of Eliahu Hakim and Eliahu Bet Tzuri, who shot to death Lord Moyne, the imperialists' "man in Cairo."

Of the Irgunists who watched with cold anger as their men were flogged and who then bared the backs of the imperialists and flogged them—and not another Jew was ever again so shamed.

Of all the names of the heroes that we need not search for in the ranks of the Vietcong or Cubans. All our lovely and shining Jews who gave of themselves so that we might live and so that the Jewish people might free itself of its oppressors and its Galut, to return home. Of all the names that we must burn forever into the hearts of our youth: Shlomo Ben Yosef, Dov Gruner, Eliezer Kashani, Eliahu Hakim, Eliahu Bet Tzuri, Yachiel Dresner, Mordechai Alkashi, Moshe Barazani, Meir Feinstein, Meir Nakar, Yakov Weiss, Avshalom Habib.

Can one now begin to understand the miracle that is the existence of the Jewish people? It is this stubbornness, this obstinate faith that never for a moment wavered, that adds yet another dimensions to *hadar*, Jewish pride. That dimension is *bitachon*—faith in the indestructibility of the Jewish people. We believe with perfect faith that the Jewish people is indestructible. A people which has suffered the cruelty, the oppression, and the Holocausts of the long night of Exile which has descended for so many centuries upon it and which, nevertheless, survived each and every one of its more powerful enemies, cannot be destroyed. It is this firm belief that is echoed every year at the Passover Seder table:

In every generation they rise up to destroy us but the Holy One, blessed be he, rescues us from their hands.

"Can these bones live?" the Prophet Ezekiel was asked as he beheld the vision of a valley filled with dry and dead Jewish bones.
And a million voices cry out: "They can and do and shall!" This is *bitachon*.

And this survival is accomplished without allies. In the end, at times of crisis, there are no allies for the Jew. Who can the Jew ultimately trust? None but himself. To whom can he look for assurance and guarantees? Only to himself and his Divine Protector. This is enough to assure Jewish survival. That is enough to swell our hearts with *hadar*.

And because of these and all the unsung and unknown Jews, who gave their lives *al kiddush a-shem* (to sanctify his Name), and who made up the oldest and most persistent national liberation movement in history, we survive today in our own state.

Our major task today is to recognize the greatness and uniqueness of the Jewish people; to recognize it, define it, and teach it unto our children; to let them know the magnificent destiny of the Jewish people.

There is a Jewish destiny that will not be denied despite all efforts to deflect it, to destroy it or to change it. The Jewish destiny is inexorable and irresistible and overcomes the gentile enemy from without and its Jewish opponent from within. How many Greeces and Romes and Churches have come and gone, while the Jewish people and their Judaism continue to exist. How many Jewish sects of Baal and how many Sadducees and Karaites and Reformers have risen up and been swept away into the junkheap of history while Judaism, the same, eternal, traditional Judaism of our fathers, continues to survive. How many Borochows and Syrkins and Brenners were there in the past and will there be in the future to create their own brand of Jewishness, and how they will all fade away and be forgotten as anything but historical footnotes. But the Jewish people together with traditional Judaism and its teaching lives and exists, chosen for destiny.

Let us shout it loud enough for our young Jews to hear and be proud. Let us repeat it enough so that we ourselves really believe. Let us patiently but determinedly create a true and honestly Jewish people and state, according to the basic concepts of Jewish thought:

1. The Jewish people is a unique and separate people, divinely chosen at Sinai as a religio-nation, transcending the shallow secular nationalism that merely divides without raising up.

2. There is a Jewish challenge: to learn, to uphold, and to teach the uniqueness of Torah that raises man to heights above the most sublime of heavenly creatures, that preaches the holiness, majesty, and divinity of man as expressed through justice, mercy, and love for all.

3. The Jewish people is one and indivisible and every Jewish brother and sister everywhere in the world is an indisoluble part of that one entity. There devolves upon each Jew the obligation to feel the physical pain and sufferings of every other Jew and to rush to his aid with all means of salvation, just as it is his duty to reach out to his spiritually ignorant and lost brothers who have wandered into strange fields and drunk from strange wells, to teach them the words of Judaism and the bonds of Jewishness.

4. While the Jew is part of Man, he is also chosen for separate existence so that he may never lose the truth that was given him; His primary loyalty lies with

The Chosen People: Definitions 109

the Jewish people and their interests take precedence over all others. We reject the Marxist concept of class struggle that divides us. The Jew has no permanent allies and he can look to no one but himself for help on this earth. The yardstick in judging all actions must be: Is it good for the Jew?

5. The home of the Jewish people is in the Land of Israel, while the Exile, in all its forms and states, must inevitably lead either to spiritual assimilation or physical destruction. Thus it is the duty of all Jews to return home, both in order to save the Jewish body and soul as well as to live a holy and Jewish life in the holy Jewish state. The Jewish state is not one more Levantine or Balkan entity but a receptacle for unique destiny.

6. The Land of Israel is the home of the Jewish people and of no one else; there has never been a Palestine or Palestinian people and never will be. The non-Jew is welcome to live in the Jewish state as an individual but not as a sovereign people, for the boundaries of Israel are those indicated in the Bible and Eretz Yisroel cannot be divided.

7. The State of Israel that arises in the Land of Israel is not a western state or an eastern one; it is not a "secular" state; it is not one to be modeled after "the nations." It is a *Jewish* state with all the uniqueness that this implies. It is a state whose personality, character, behavior, and structure must be the reflection of Jewishness and Judaism.

These are the reasons for being different, the reasons for separation and separate growth and nationality. Not a perverted sense of a master race that reproduces the horrors of Nazism; not the desire to conquer foreign lands and rule over peoples; not a hunger for power, wealth, cruel domination; rather a challenge to ourselves, a demand that we be holier, more spiritual, more ready to sacrifice. This is Jewish uniqueness.

If our youth are not given reasons for being Jewish, they will loosen and cut their ties with world Jews, with whom they will see little in common; they will cast off Jewishness and Judaism as irrelevant if not backward and harmful to world integration, amalgamation, and brotherhood. And there will follow all the practical consequences of which we spoke earlier: the lowering of the barriers to intermarriage and assimilation; the increase in emigration from Israel to the lands of prosperity; the secularization of the state and its splitting into two separate camps of two separate peoples; identification with the Arab struggle and the willingness to accept "peace" that is really suicide; and an increase in materialism, moral anarchy, class and communal hatred, and vicious crime.

Jewish values and Jewish uniqueness must be brought into the schools and the indoctrination of our children in their heritage must be made the aim of education in Israel. Hopefully, our youth will understand the need to practice their Judaism. But even if the individual Jew feels that it is too difficult for him, let him at least have teachers who present the truth in a positive way. Let him at least have an opportunity to see the depth and greatness of his faith and heritage. Let him at least realize that even if he cannot practice it, the Jewish nation and state must be shaped, colored, and identified through it. When the Jewish child is taught the concept of the divine election of his people and the uniqueness that is his heritage, he will develop the pride and sense of responsibility that will keep him a loyal and devoted Jew. *Hadar, hadar atzmi*—self-pride. This is what we must give each of the Jewish children of destiny.

5

The Chosen State: The Jew Without

The State of Israel does not exist in a vacuum. It is not merely one more sovereign state in a world of sovereign states, each obligated only to its citizens—those who carry its passport, who are liable to its laws and regulations, who are within the actual boundaries of its territory or on temporary leave from it. The State of France is concentric with the citizens of France. The Frenchman who emigrates to the United States and takes out American citizenship, gives up his French citizenship and his French nationality (he remains a man of French "descent," a vague concept).

Not so with the State of Israel. It is not concentric with the citizens of Israel. It is not concerned only with the Israeli Jew who lives within the state and who carries the Israeli identity card. Israel is the land of the Jewish people, the Jewish state, and its ties to Jews wherever they may be, what ever land they may be citizens of, remain unbroken. It has a right to demand certain things of them and it has firm and definite obligations to them, for the Jewish people throughout the world is one people and its ultimate home is in the Land of Israel, under a sovereign Jewish state. What I am saying is that the Jewish people and the Land of Israel are involved in a dual relationship that is eternal. The people, both within and without the land, owe it allegiance; the land owes them duties and exists only as the servant of the people.

This is not to say that the Jew outside of Israel is not a citizen of the country that grants him citizenship. He is. It is not to say that he is a citizen of Israel when he has not requested it. He is not. But while the Jew in exile must serve with loyalty the country in which he resides, the fact remains that the Jewish people throughout the world is one people and that the ties between Jews are not like the ties between men of French descent. They are firmer, permanent and unbreakable. The Jew owes his allegiance to the state in which he lives, which has given him benefits and which calls him its citizen. But, unlike others who descend from nations that occupy a different territory, who have left those lands, and who have little if any ties to them the Jew is different.

The Jew is part of a nation whose existence is independent of any state. When there was no Jewish state, there was still a Jewish nation who were bound to the Land of Israel, and now that there is a Jewish state there is still a Jewish nation whether it lives within that state or outside it. Moreover, it is the obligation of every Jew to go and live in that state; this has been the hope of the Jewish people, as expressed in Judaism, its prayers and commandments. Thus, while the Jew may still live outside the borders of Israel, he does not lose his obligation to the Land of Israel, whether there is a state there or not. So long as his duty to the Land of Israel does not conflict with his duty to the land in which he temporarily resides, he must do all in his power to aid the Land of the Jews. When that duty does come into conflict he must leave the land, give up his citizenship, and resolve the conflict by returning from Exile to his permanent home, the Land of Israel.

The Jew outside of the Land of Israel lives in Exile. It does not matter whether he considers it so or not. (Truth is never dependent upon subjective belief, especially when that belief is the illusion of foolish people.) His home is the Land of Israel, whether there is a Jewish state or not. His obligation is to that Land (he prays for rain for the Land of Israel) and his obligation is to go up to that Land. (No political Zionism can ever match the religious obligation to go and live in the Land, for it is the religion that created a concept of Zion in the first place). The fact that the Jew does not return to Zion in no way frees him from the obligation or from the need to do all that is necessary to aid those who do live there.

If a Jewish state comes into existence in the Land of Israel, that state has a right to call upon all Jews for support. It is not charity or the goodness of the Jew in Exile that is in question here. One aids the needy of Africa or Asia or any foreign state because one understands the moral obligation to help a human being in need. But the Jew aids the Jewish state or the people who live in the Land of Israel because it is the Jewish home, because it is his obligation to, because it is his. An appeal for funds for Israel is not an appeal for funds for India. The one is a call for a stranger and the other is an obligation toward one's own. One *should* help the stranger, one must help his own.

The obligation of the Jew in Exile to the Land of Israel, and to any sovereign Jewish state therein, is unimpeachable, no matter how difficult this may be for those Jews who have persuaded themselves that their Exile citizenship has cut all but fraternal ties with the Land of the Jews.

But the relationship between the Jew in Exile and the Jewish Land is not one-sided. If the Jew in Exile is obliged to aid the Land, the Land is obliged to look upon itself as the guardian, the trustee, the spokesman, the defender of the Jew throughout the world.

The State of Israel has at times recognized this concept. At other times it has ignored it or swerved from it. When the question of German reparations arose and West Germany obligated itself to pay hundreds of millions of dollars for Jewish property confiscated and destroyed, the State of Israel demanded—and the Germans agreed to—the recognition of the Jewish state as the guardian and spokesman of the European Jews who were destroyed. And if there are those who say that this guardianship holds true only for dead Jews and that Israel is merely their executor, let us point to yet another shining affirmation of the true role of the Jewish state, in its judgment of Adolph Eichmann.

Surely, a state that was not in existence at the time that Eichmann's crimes took place and which laid no claim to the citizenship of those victims had no "legal" right to try Eichmann. Yet it was the moral claim of guardianship and trusteeship over the Jewish people that was Israel's argument and brief to the world. Eichmann was tried before a court of the Jewish state because he attempted to wipe out the Jewish people; he was hanged by the Jewish state because he tried to wipe out the Jewish nation. The Jewish state stands as representative of the Jewish nation whether it existed at the time of the crime, whether the nation or any part of it asks for its aid, or whether any part of the Jewish people disassociates itself from a relationship to people or state.

It is in this role of trustee and guardian that the State of Israel comes to the Jewish people and seeks monetary support or demands manpower through Aliya. It does not come and merely ask for that aid. If it did, it would not concentrate primarily on Jews. When the Israeli or the United Jewish Appeal speaker approaches his Jewish audience, it is not on the same basis as he would a bank or a wealthy Christian. To these there is either an appeal unrelated to obligation or a business approach unconnected with emotion. Not so with the Jewish audience.

Here, there is more than business and more than charity: there is obligation. You are Jews, cries the Israeli, and this is the home for which we prayed for two thousand years. You are Jews, and this is our answer to the anti-Semites. You are Jews and this is the Jewish state. Give because you *should* give; what kind of a Jew does not support his own?

And the Jew in Los Angeles or London or Brisbane or Paris or Johannesburg listens and nods agreement. And gives. But is that all there is to the relationship? If the Jew in Exile owes it to the Jewish state to defend it, because he is a Jew, does not the Jewish State owe it to him to defend him because it is a Jewish state? If the Jew in London gives of himself to the Jewish state, is it not incumbent on the Jewish state to give of itself to him? Indeed, no Jewish government can avoid its obligation and turn the relationship of the Israeli and the exile into a one-way street.

It is not what is good for Israel that must determine the foreign policy of the Jewish state but what is good for the Jewish people, no matter what difficulties this may cause for the Foreign Ministry. Thus if the vociferous outcries by Israel and the Zionist movement against the Soviet Union's policy on Jews conflicts with hopes for closer ties between Israel and the Kremlin, the ties must take a back seat to the needs of the Soviet Jews. We have yet to hear the entire story of official Israeli passivity and efforts to quiet militant and not-so-militant protests on behalf of Soviet Jewry because it was felt that the interests of the state would be harmed.

An Israeli foreign policy that recognizes its obligation as trustee of the interests of the entire Jewish people is a foreign policy that does not hesitate to "interfere" in the affairs of a United States in order to assure that legislation which will aid Soviet Jewry will pass in Congress. It does not hesitate to go against the stand of an American President whom it otherwise needs, in order to save Soviet Jews. Phantom jets for Israel are important but not at the expense of Jews within the Soviet Union and whenever the possibility of our risking Israeli interests comes up against the certainty of loss of world Jewish interests then the latter must take priority.

Similarly, such a foreign policy makes no distinction between the endangered Israeli Jew and the endangered "foreign" Jew. If we permit ourselves to force down a Lebanese airliner because we believe that terrorist leader George Habash is aboard, knowingly violating international law by removing him, why is the same airliner allowed to leave with the Iraqi Ambassador untouched at the very moment four hundred Iraqi Jews in Baghdad continue to live in terror, unable to leave that country? If we allow ourselves to "eliminate" terrorists in Cyprus, Rome, and Paris, why does the Israeli government not allow itself to act against Syrian officials who hold four thousand Jews in a virtual prison and under inhuman conditions?

The answer is, of course, that in the one case it is Israelis who are endangered by Arab terrorists while in the other, "just" Jews are threatened by their respective governments. That answer, I bluntly say, is unacceptable and unworthy of a Jewish government and a truly Jewish foreign policy.

The State of Israel is under deep moral and Jewish obligation to look upon itself as the guardian and trustee of the Jewish people wherever they may be and to follow a foreign policy that places Jewish interests first. This has not always been so, even in the case of the interests of Israeli citizens—and here I refer to the shameful refusal of the state to ban the increasing and scandalous Christian missionary activity within Israel, ostensibly on the grounds that in a democracy such a thing cannot be done. Yet the government has been quick enough to "modify" the democratic process when it has felt that the situation warranted. The reason given for such actions is usually "security," and I do not strongly argue with that. But surely security reasons that limit democracy are no more compelling for Jews than the need to stop missionaries from snatching Jewish souls.

The real reason for Israeli refusal to stop missionaries is fear of a Church outcry: in the United Nations, where a Vatican protest might endanger the Catholic Latin American vote; and in the United States, whose large Fundamentalist Protestant groups have descended in missionary droves on the Jewish state. These and other examples are blots on the garment of the Jewish state and blatant contradictions in the role of Israel vis-a-vis the Jewish people.

Israel's role as guardian of the Jewish people calls for a tough, "brazen" foreign policy. It calls for it to cry out strongly against oppression of Jews everywhere and to "interfere" in the internal affairs of a state that oppresses Jews, if need be. It calls for vigorous Israeli leadership in urging Jewish groups in all countries to demonstrate and protest meaningfully. It calls for action on behalf of Jews even if it means treading on the toes of people whose support Israel feels it needs.

Thus, if Arab terror becomes a real and meaningful thing—which it is—it is inexcusable for a Jewish government to disassociate itself from any aid to Jews who are targets of the terror, on the grounds that they are not Israeli citizens. There can be no distinction between Israeli Jew and non-Israeli Jew when either is a target *because he is a Jew.* If his Jewishness makes him a target, then the Jewish state must exercise its rule as the Jewish protector. It must do for the Jew in Exile what it demands that he do for it—especially when he has become a target precisely because of his aid for the Jewish state.

It is worse than foolish to beg the nations of the world to fight the Jewish cause and to protect their Jewish citizens from attack. It is foolish because the nations will do a perfunctory job at best. But it is also immoral. The Jewish state is the trustee of Jews not only when it stands to benefit from that relationship; it is their trustee in obligation, too.

Therefore, if there is a need to organize Jewish groups in the Exile, to train them, to arm them, to support them, to supply them, and to give them haven, the Jewish state must fulfill that need. And if even more is required, namely the use of Israeli men and supplies to protect Jewish lives that are not being protected by

The Chosen State: The Jew Without 121

anyone—so be it. Israel cannot free itself of the responsibility of meeting anti-Semitic outrages in the Exile that grow and threaten the existence of Jews.

And if Aliya becomes more than merely a benefit to Israel but also a desperate need for Jews of a particular country, there is an obligation on the part of Israeli messengers to speak bluntly about the growth of Jew hatred in that country without fear of inviting either the displeasure of the host country or the wrath of the Jewish Establishment there. I refer specifically to countries such as Argentina and the United States. In the former—and to a lesser extent in a number of other Latin countries—the political atmosphere is fraught with tension. The revolution in Cuba marked something far different than the usual overthrow by junta of the government. The drastic social and economic upheaval taking place in Latin America bodes ill for the Jew, who is a target not only because of his religious and racial differences. It is no longer just the Right that seeks Jewish blood. Now it is the Left that looks upon him as an economic target, a mainstay of the capitalist, bourgeois system. Yet the Israelis in charge of Aliya hesitate to openly and frantically cry out the danger.

The situation is even sadder in the United States, where the American Jew refuses, even more than the Latin American, to see the danger and where the wealthy Establishment, which pours so much money into Israel, reacts with great hostility to any mention of the need for emergency Aliya. (Surely this is the reason why the Zionist Congress in 1972 refused to allow the subject to be broached. Surely it was not because the Israelis there did not wish to hear about it, but because the American delegates—who hold the purse strings—were adamant in their refusal).

Yet the danger is a very real one. Six million American Jews (once *again* the figure) stand in real danger of a growing wave of Jew-hatred in a country that, with all its democratic past and history of freedom, is a cruel and violent society. It is a country that has been relatively free of the Old World clashes between groups because until recently it had a vast frontier that gave opportunity and employment to those who came there. For the most part, the competition that bred the hatred for the Jew in Europe was not felt in this young country that allowed expansion and opportunity. But things have changed. The past twenty-five American years, apparently so free of overt Jew-hatred, were an illusion. There were two major reasons for this illusion, both of which are no longer valid.

The terrible Holocaust that shocked the world with its horrors thirty years ago created a temporary embargo on anti-Semitism. The Jew buys the favor of the world with his bodies, and the destruction of six million Jews made the anti-Semite a temporary pariah.

Added to this was the unprecedented economic boom that brought the good life to America and allowed it to wallow in automobiles, private homes, full employment, and consumer luxuries undreamed of before. Anti-Semites have slim pickings during good times: a steak in the broiler and a new automobile in the garage dilute the appeal of the hater. The guilt of Auschwitz and the good economic times saw anti-Semitism arrested, but not eliminated. But today both these factors, have undergone fundamental change and no longer serve as a barrier to the resurgence of virulent Jew-hatred.

The guilt of Auschwitz is gone. Time and the victories of Israel in battle have enabled the gentile to rid himself of his albatross. On the other hand, the days of economic boom have ended for the United States and the good life has been replaced by one that has sounds of ugliness and danger.

America is today a troubled land, torn by racial passions and hatreds. We find white pitted against black in anger over the busing of children to achieve integration, violence over changing neighborhoods and housing patterns, competition for blue-collar and low-level white-collar jobs, tension and fighting between races in schools and in the armed forces. The fact that cities are not burning or that progress has been made by minorities fools only the foolish. Today extremists are taking over the cities intact as the middle class flees from them like the plague, while progress that has been made leads only to rising expectations and escalated demands for more. And who will be blamed for all this if not the Jew, whose presence in the civil rights movement was so prominent? Who, if not the liberal Jew, will be the major target of embittered masses of Americans?

Then there is the defeat of the United States in Vietnam—and let there be no mistake, it is a defeat. Who will be blamed for the humiliation and the needless deaths? Who will be saddled with the myth of a war that might have been won if not for "the stab in the back?" The war that has poisoned America and split it into hostile camps, that has embittered the military and maligned armed forces leadership, will be blamed on the Jew who, again, was so prominent in opposition to the war. Long after Americans have forgotten the names of McGovern and McCarthy they will remember Rubin and Hoffman, and above all Kissinger. As Weimar fell before a legend of traitors at home so is there a new myth being woven at this moment. Both have the same central villain—the Jew.

The general hostility of Middle America to the radical Left and its opposition to their long-cherished values will once again lead to hostility against those who are looked upon as the destroyers of the land. Once again, the prominence of some Jews in movements which mock and attack the flag, the office of the presidency, and the things that mean so much to the simple American will lead to a movement from the middle to the radical Right and to bitter hatred of Jews as a whole.

The frustration of the average American as he watches social, moral, and ethical values that he has long cherished, being mocked and changed is evident to all. The gap between himself and his children, the spread of pornography and the change in sexual standards, anger and frighten him. Once again he seeks a way to go back to what he considers standards of decency. Once again he yearns for people who will give him permanent values. Once again he seeks to lash out at those who he believes have been responsible for the social revolution. Once again his target is the Jew.

The Chosen State: The Jew Without 125

And on top of the racial, political, social, and psychological problems there comes the spark that could set off the powder keg upon which we sit. The land of the mighty dollar, the economic colossus, is suddenly shaken. America is confronted with millions of unemployed and an untold number of underemployed. Urban areas, already dying as welfare clients demand higher payments and the flight of the middle class dictates less revenue, become centers for joblessness that breed a staggering hate. At the same time, inflation continues to eat away at the dollar and the lower middle class watch in agonized impotence as their savings are wasted away.

For the first time in a quarter century large numbers of people face the loss of the good life they have known for so long. Such people are dangerous for they will not come to terms with poverty; they will sooner turn to demagogues and racists who will promise them the good life in return for their liberties and at the price of the scapegoat—the Jew.

And those demagogues, haters, and facists are to be found in the United States in abundance. Forget their numbers at present. Consider rather their recent growth and their capacity to grow tremendously in an era of violence, frustration, anger, bitterness, fear, and hate. These are the elements that are present in American society today and upon which the haters feed. They speak openly of gas chambers and of eliminating Jews. They mean it, and no one knows if they can really be stopped if conditions become ripe.

In the face of this a threat to six million Jews, the State of Israel must disregard all protests and make plans for a mass emergency Aliya and any other steps that are necessary. This too is part of its responsibility as the trustee of the Jewish people.

There is another area where the existence of Israel as a *Jewish* state calls for re-examination and introspection. When the idea of political Zionism flashed across European Jewry's horizon and when the first Jewish settlers came to build a Jewish home in the Land of Israel (then misnamed Palestine), they found a desolate, destroyed, and ravaged land. But they did not find an *empty* land. They found tens of thousands of Arabs, many of whose families dated back generations. It was these indigenous inhabitants that Zionism, theory and practitioners, greeted with *"Anv banv artza,"* We have come home!

To the astonished Arab's question (that would grow louder and angrier with the passage of time and the influx of more Jews): "Who are you and what right do you have to come to this land?" the Zionists had a ready answer, one that was self-evident. "We are *Jews,*" they replied, "and this is the land of our fathers to which we have come home."

There was never the slightest doubt over this answer. The Jews were coming to this strange land *by right*— because it was the home of the Jews and each and every Jew had a G-d-given, historic right that no one could deny.

No one, it seems, except other Jews.

When the State of Israel came into being, among the very first things it did was to codify its right to exist. The Law of Return! The law that underlined for our times the realization of the vision: "And may our eyes behold thy return to Zion . . ." The Law of Return that uncompromisingly gave each and every Jew the unmistakable and unshakable right to return Home.

Not just "some" Jews and not just "good" Jews. Not just "respectable" Jews and not just religious or Marxist or cultured or "acceptable" Jews. Just Jews. Including the bad, the criminal, the shameful, the disgraceful—all the Jews whom G-d made. That is what the Law of Return once spoke of—because it had to.

For to deny one Jew the right to entry was to deny the entire raison d'etre of Zionism, to falsify the entire claim of those who came into a land inhabited by Arabs.

Yet that is what has happened, as under the politicians and the diplomats, the Law of Return has become the Law of Quasi Return, of return for some and of rejection for others. The fact is that today there are many Jews who can be, and have been, barred from entering the Jewish state, have been ejected after entry, even extradited.

To be sure, there are rational reasons given. There always are. "Israel cannot be a haven for criminals. Israel, as a member of the community of nations, has international obligations and cannot allow foreign criminals to mock the law of the state in the knowledge that they can always flee here. Israel cannot allow in people with criminal records who will 'endanger' the state."

And so Israel turns away all kinds of Jews declared to be undesirable. The Jewish state—for all desirable Jews. This is what happens when politicians and diplomats begin to take themselves seriously, when an ideal begins to take a back seat to "international considerations." When the Land of Israel descends into the State of Israel.

The right of a State of Israel to exist is dependent upon the right of the Jew to a Land of Israel. The state can do nothing in denegration of the imperatives of the land. And if the decree of the Land of Israel through the Jewish heritage is that *every* Jew has a right to enter and live there, then no Knesset and no state can do anything to contradict that edict.

Here we have one more example of the corruption of the true meaning of the State of Israel vis-a-vis the Jewish people. Instead of an affirmation of the Jewish people as an indivisible nation with each and every Jew entitled to the same rights from the Jewish state, we find that there are indeed "Jews" and "Israelis." The criminal born in Tel Aviv is not deported from Israel, but the one who tries to enter the land from Chicago is. A 72-year-old "foreign" criminal becomes a "danger to the state," but a native-born Communist whose allegiance is to Moscow is not. A "foreign" Jew who is deemed "undesirable" cannot live in the Land of Israel but hundreds of thousands of Arabs can. Maybe this is good western, liberal thinking, proper democratic, nation-state logic —but it is terrible Judaism. This is what happens when the State of Israel loses its way in the world, when it forgets that it came into being as the servant of the Jewish people, that it is the latter's agent and trustee. This is Israel with the first rot of assimilation upon it.

I do not suggest that there is an easy answer to Jewish criminals coming to Israel to seek safety from punishment. I am sure that, given a little effort, "a Jew finds a solution." If we are unhappy with the entering Jewish criminal or undesirable, let us punish him, jail him, even hang him. But let us not bar his entry or deport him. And above all, let us not commit that most abominable and un-Jewish of crimes, extradition to a foreign, non-Jewish state. We have had enough disillusioning examples of Israeli cooperation with foreign gentiles in the matter of Jewish criminals, *including those whose "crimes" consist of attacking the Soviets or Arabs on behalf of Jews.*

Would such a new policy cause us difficulties in the community of nations? Perhaps. Would it cause uncomfortable moments for the Foreign Minister? It might very well. No matter. The Jewish state did not come into being to make life easier for the Jewish Foreign Minister (and let us always remember that he is the *Jewish* foreign minister). Israel came into being on behalf of Jews, *all* the world's Jews, and not to worry over "What will the nations say?"

Let the Israeli government know and let us, the citizens of Israel and particularly the most fortunate of all people, those who were born here, know also. The Land of Israel is not the province of the Israeli alone. It belongs to each and every Jew, and each and every Jew has a right to come here, to speak up or down, for or against. There are no Israelis and Jews—there are only Jews.

And let every Jew in Israel who rejects this contention and who bellows forth, "I am an Israeli, not a Jew" know that he is a thief. For such a man has indeed stolen this land from the Arabs who lived here before he or his father arrived. It was not as Israelis that we told the Arabs that this is our land, that we have come home. It was only as Jews, as the descendants of those who had wandered through Exile never forgetting the dream of Zion, and those descendants in turn were the descendants of those who had once lived in Zion. As Jews we have *all* rights in this land. As people who reject Jewishness and create an "Israeliness," we have nothing. We are indeed thieves.

The Jew in America is first a Jew. The Jew in Israel is first a Jew. Both the one in America and the one in the Land who deny this are stricken with the same guilt mentality and inferiority complex. They both seek to escape from their unique and difficult heritage. Yet there is no escape from the truth of one Jewish people and the one state which is their home and which owes them inseparable support just as it demands from them inseparable obligation.

We are grappling here with the questions: What is the purpose of Zionism's creation of a Jewish State? Why does the State of Israel exist? Depending on the answers one gives, he will create a certain kind of state.

If the reason given is so that the Jews might save themselves from anti-Semitism, might "normalize" themselves and be as other peoples and states, there will certainly emerge a very definite kind of state. It will, indeed, be like all others and conform to the international game. It will look upon itself as sovereign, committed to the "good" of the state and its citizens, loyal to the western concept of democracy, of the sovereignty and exclusiveness of the state and the citizens within it, with all that this implies for its citizens of all nationalities. In many crucial areas it will separate itself from the non-Israeli Jew, as we have seen, and it will follow diplomatic and political permutations and combinations with consequences that are often at variance with the traditional concept of a single, unified Jewish people.

A "normal" state, one that is like other nations, cannot think in terms of protecting Jews who are citizens or other states. The rules of the international community will not allow it to harbor Jewish criminals, and the democratic ideal will not tolerate the banning of a Christian mission—in the end it will decree that a ban on intermarriage must also be laid aside. Surely, its obligation to the Israeli Christian or Muslim will come before any duty to a "foreign" Jew. Certainly, fear of interfering in the internal affairs of another state—especially if it is a friendly one and even more especially if it is one whose help and support we need—will prevent the "normal" state from making statements or carrying on activities concerning Jewish citizens of that state. Certainly, what is good for the state will take precedence over what is good for the universal Jewish people.

But if one looks at the raison d'être for a Jewish state from a Jewish standpoint; if one sees it within the context of its role in the total Jewish scheme of life; if one looks upon it as a tool for Jewish existence, Jewish identity, and Jewish heritage, to aid Jews in need in the Galut and to serve as the place where all Jews can lead a full Jewish life; as a servant of the Jewish people—then one creates a different kind of state.

Then one postulates a State of Israel in the service of world Jewry, which bases its policies on what is good for all Jews, those within the state and those without. Then one describes a state that is chained to the great foundation of Jewish foundations, Ahavat Yisroel, the love for each and every Jew.

What is Ahavat Yisroel? How does one define it and, more important, how does one attain it?

The story has come down to us of the Yom Kippur when, with the day drawing to a close and the fast leaving him weak and drawn, Rabbi Levi Yitzchak of Berdishev rose and spoke to his Maker:

G-d of Abraham, Isaac, and Jacob, you constantly admonish us to walk in your footsteps, but why do you not, once in a while, cleave to some of our ways? When a Jew accidentally lets slip his tefillin *(phylacteries) from his hand, he hastens to pick them up, kisses them tenderly, and fasts that day, such is his love for your* tefillin.

You, however, who, as our rabbis tell us, wear tefillin *that read, "And who is like thy people Israel, one nation on earth," have taken that* tefillin, *that people of Israel, and cast them to the earth, thrown them down from the great pinnacle of freedom and happiness they once knew, to the dust of exile and persecution.*

And there they have lain for close to two thousand years and you do not even bother to lift them up to kiss them or to fast over them. If you will forgive your tefillin *and pick them up and forgive them, it is well.*

But if not, I will be forced to tell the world that the Almighty dons improper tefillin.

And the Hasidic legend continues that these words of Rabbi Levi Yitzchak reached up to the very Throne of Glory, to the Holy One blessed be he, himself, who smiled and said, "You have won, my son Levi Yitzchak. I forgive them as you have spoken.

This is Ahavat Yisroel from one who felt it and lived it. And we can only sadly recognize its magnificence and beauty as we look at our orphaned generation and behold its absence. One can appreciate light only after being trapped in Stygian darkness.

While six million died and news of the extermination camps emerged before a horrified Jewish world, our Jewish leadership, which did indeed love and care for Jews, nevertheless did not love them enough. It did not possess that burning passion and feeling heart that gave a sense of urgency and immediacy to their mission. How far we were from the heights of a Levi Yitzchak! It is not that we failed to anticipate their destruction. It was worse. When they cried out, we were paralyzed, and when they sought our help, we were frozen into that worst of all postures, impotency.

The failure of world Jewry to do for their own brothers and sisters threatened with extermination what they were prepared to do in later years for all kinds of strange causes and peoples is a permanent stain on the Jewish soul. We can never say, with any degree of honesty, *Yadeinu lo shafchu et ha-dam ha-ze* ("Our hands have not had a share in the shedding of this blood").

This is what happens when one does not possess Ahavat Yisroel to the degree that it pushes, drives, obsesses, and gives no rest to the Jew as long as another Jew needs him. The Holocaust is the prime example, in our times, of lack of Ahavat Yisroel.

For Ahavat Yisroel is the understanding that there is one Jewish people, indivisible and eternal, with each and every Jew a permanent part of it and with duty to people as a cornerstone of personal Jewish existence. To love the Jewish brother and sister with all your heart and with all your soul and with all your means. And what is true for the Jew as an individual is true for the Jewish state. It, too, must learn Ahavat Yisroel and practice it.

Both individual Jew and Jewish state must believe and practice that the Jewish people are not only a unique people but a separate people with total rejection of the Marxist call for class struggle that divides the nation into warring camps and decrees that the fate of the Jewish worker lies with the gentile worker against the Jewish employer. This is a philosophy of the Galut, the Exile, a philosophy that is un-Jewish and that must be uprooted from the Jewish mind. Jewish problems can be solved only within a Jewish framework, and the Jewish worker and employer are part of the separate and unique Jewish nation. All Jews are brothers and the non-Jew is apart and separate from this relationship. And let it be shouted forth that the Jew in Israel is bound by ties to the Jew in the Galut that are infinitely greater and incomparable to anything that he holds in common with the non-Jew who is an Israeli citizen. This is the honest meaning of "Thou hast chosen us from all the peoples" and "He

The Chosen State: The Jew Without 135

who separates Israel from the nations." Upon this principle the policies and programs of a Jewish state must be based.

Both Jew and Jewish state must learn that, for them, there are no permanent allies among the non-Jews. The states must realize that, at best, we can expect from the non-Jew only short-range support, a support based on the self-interest of the parties to the relationship. At no time can this short-range, temporary support be a moral or a logical reason for betraying or ignoring Jewish interests.

Both Jew and Jewish state must understand that in formulating policies, the measuring rod to be used at all times is: Is it good for the Jews? It is time to stop being more Catholic than the Pope and to understand that on questions of foreign policy it is not our "fraternal ties" with the Third World or our efforts to curry favor with the revolutionary Left that must dictate our policies but, simply, whether it is good for the Jews. There can be no dichotomy, no division of loyalties between Judaism and any other "ism." If the socialist Jew finds it difficult to support the United States, when that is vital to Jewish interests, that is his problem. A good Jew asks only if support for anything will aid the Jew. Our alliances in the world must be based not only on the principle of *kabdehu v chashdehu* ("respect but suspect") but also on our pragmatic ability to back any (except the truly evil and immoral) state whose interests coincide with our own—at that moment.

It is Jewish interests that come first for Jews, not socialist or capitalist ones. It is the Jewish people that is the touchstone, not Third World or Fourth World, ad infinitum. Our loyalties lie neither with Moscow nor Peking nor Washington. They lie with the universal Jewish people. The Jewish government of the Jewish state within the Land of Israel is the servant of world Jewry, just as world Jewry is obligated to support, strive for, and live within its own state. The policies of that government must be based on this hypothesis.

Israel's policy, domestic and foreign, must be one that rejects the too-relevant ghetto mentality that always looks over its diplomatic shoulder to see "what the nations will say." It must be a policy that is dynamic, tough, even "brazen," seeking not to impress people or to buy friendship with cautious steps, but to make it clear to the world that Israel will do *whatever* is necessary for its people, the Jewish people. It must be one that rejects the siren call of "practicality" and "reality" over vision and ideal. It is time that we learned that, in the end, the "practical" policy that betrays idealistic vision proves to be impractical, while the "impractical" people and policies of bold imagination are the only practical ones.

It is only when we understand and act upon the understanding that the Land of Israel (and the state within it) is the trustee and agent of world Jewish interests, that we will cease betraying Zionism, the reason for being of the State of Israel, the true relationship between the Jewish state and the Jewish people, and Ahavat Yisroel as well.

How do a Jewish people and state express their uniqueness, their Jewishness? by their external character alone? No, there is more. There are unique ideas in Judaism, unique ways of looking at problems, unique ways of deciding how to behave and how to react. If a people and state are truly Jewish, their standards and their value judgments will be Jewish ones, nothing else. Whether a thing is right or wrong, whether it should be done or not done, said or not said, will be decided not by western or eastern, liberal or conservative, socialist or capitalist, democratic or autocratic standards, but by Jewish ones.

In the end, true faith in the state as the beginning of the redemption is lacking even among the religious. Few are there, indeed, who are prepared to give up the "logical," "practical," and "rational" approach to problems facing Israel. Fearful of world opinion, of numbers, of armies, and of diplomatic pressures, nearly all of us have fallen prey to a fear that limits our actions, that drives us from the way of boldness and truth—from Jewish reactions.

Will the Americans approve? Will the Russians be angry? Will the Christian world react? Will Africans, Asians, and the United Nations condemn? These are the questions that make up the Galut mentality of too many in Israel and that drive government and politicians to shrink from doing and not doing things according to Jewish values.

The cornerstone of Jewish foreign policy must be the knowledge and faith that the Jewish people have a divine destiny that cannot be denied and that the State of Israel is the culmination of that destiny. It must be based on the realization that our G-d is the G-d of history and it is within his hands that the fate of nations is decided. If a decision must be taken that affects the lives of the

Jewish people, the future of their state, or the destiny of both, that decision must be a bold one that calls for both sacrifice and strength of arms as well as a deep and abiding faith that so long as the Jew remains true to his people and destiny, he can never be defeated.

It is only people who lack such a faith who become politicans and diplomats, who shrink from the seemingly difficult, and who find refuge in "logic" and "reason." It is only Jews of little or no faith who decide to forego a pre-emptive strike that would save the lives of hundreds of Jewish soldiers, with the argument that the political climate forces Israel to moderate its policy for fear of what the world will say and do.

Jewish foreign policy must never be built upon the same transient and finite assumptions of others. We are not a "natural" people but a G-dly one and our belief in the Jewish G-d of history must create within us a faith in the inevitable victory of the Jew who remains faithful to his destiny.

We must cease fearing sanctions and isolation in the world community for it is not from the world community that salvation will come. We must stop measuring our strength in terms of numbers or quality, for Israel is saved not through finite man but through infinite G-d.

What is needed is courage and assurance that we are a people whose G-d will give us strength and might to overcome all our enemies—if only we follow the Jewish way of action and reaction. What we need is true belief—not mere lip service—that we are on the threshold of the final liberation. What we need is to believe that the events of our time are indeed miracles that herald a redemption that no one on earth—nation, group, or army—can ever stem. It is only with the deeply felt belief that "these may come with chariots and these with horses but we shall invoke the name of the Eternal, our G-d" that we shall ignore the "logical" way of the diplomats and remain true to the one continuous path of Ahavat Yisroel, the doing of whatever is necessary to help our fellow Jews, and ourselves regardless of what the world may say.

6

The Chosen State: The Jew Within

Where is Ahavat Yisroel needed more than inside the State of Israel? Where more than here do we need more dialogue, tolerance, understanding, love, and compassion for those among us?

We speak of the social gap and yet how sad it is that, on the one hand, there are those who have never entered a poverty neighborhood or who pay lip service to the problems of the stricken and then soothe their consciences by repeating the easy formula that there is not enough money for both defense and poverty. And on the other hand are those who are either too simple to understand or too demagogic to want to allow others to understand the terrible complexity of the problem and who wallow in cynical charges of racism and callous communal hatred. Both camps are sitting on a powder keg, the one believing it will somehow disappear, thus allowing them to continue to enjoy the good life, the other, in full knowledge if its existence, playing with lighted matches.

The need to allocate funds to the poor and deprived of Israel is obvious. Everyone knows and talks about it; few do anything about it.

It is not true that all-out efforts have been made to raise large amounts of funds to fight poverty, to create schools, and to cater to the basic needs of the deprived. They have certainly not been presented to the world Jewish public with the same earnestness and sense of urgency as drives for warplanes. No real sense of emergency has been conveyed to the wealthy Jewish communities of the world.

Nor have the Jews of the world given all that they might possibly be expected to give. One can indeed stand in awe at the vast sums of money given by western Jews to the various appeals from Israel, but only when one looks upon them from the basis of relativity. Yes, relative to the gentile the Jew gives an extraordinary amount of money to charity and to Israel. Yes, relative to the standard of living in Israel, a man who gives what the American or South African or Swiss Jew gives, does indeed deserve to be praised. But when one considers how many Jews in the West have never given at all, and what a relatively small percentage of their fortune so many have given, and that the western Jew really has no idea of the extent of the poverty in Israel and its explosive implications—then quite a different picture emerges.

More money, much more money, could be gotten from world Jewry if the appeal were made in the form of a separate emergency fund or surcharge on the regular contribution. The pity is that this has not been done and that a sense of urgency has not been communicated to world Jewry by the government of Israel. The need to allocate vast funds for the needy is obvious, yet little more than little has been done to enlist the vast resources of world Jewry.

Similarly, to castigate the government for its relative indifference to the need to eliminate waste, bureaucratic rot, scandals, and corruption is also obvious — to all but the government. Few have any real idea what the scandals in governmental circles have cost the state — money that could and should be used for bridging the social gap.

As one who loves his Land of Israel deeply, I write these words with pain. It is utterly irrelevant that one can find the same waste and corruption, or worse, in other countries. I do not want to see it in my land. Nor is this criticism intended to do anything but convince the Jew of the Land to make things better and the Jew of the Exile to come here and create a better state. Mine is not the criticism of the spies of Canaan but of the rabbis who say: "Any love that is not accompanied by criticism is not real love."

We have seen too much of the government's indifference to public opinion in its unwillingness to delve into scandals and to punish the Labor Party activists connected with them. This indifference stems from the certain knowledge that on election day the public will put the Labor Party back in office as they have done every time since the beginning of the state and for years before that. And here is a danger that we must face frankly.

No democracy in the world can "boast" of such a phenomenon of unbroken political power. It carries within itself a threat to the democracy of Israel that cannot be overestimated. If, as Lord Acton said, power corrupts and absolute power corrupts absolutely, we have a clear danger of this in Israel.

For absolute power, along with the absolute certainty that it will continue, leads to an absolute arrogance and corruption that will not end until the individuals concerned know that they can be thrown out. It also leads to a determination on their part not to be thrown out, so that they are prepared to do immoral things in order to assure their continued stay in power. Nowhere is this desire to preserve power at all costs seen more clearly than in the root cause of the terrible social and communal gap that everyone deplores.

While it is true that proverty is a tragedy and must be fought, this poverty cannot be looked at outside of the total context in which it emerged. Poverty is not the root cause of the communal gap or of the crime, social upheaval, materialist values, and destruction of moral standards that come in its wake. All the things that we see growing in the poverty areas of Israel—the prostitution, the thievery, the hooliganism—do not arise from poverty itself. They stem from a deep loss of moral and social values, values that were held by Jews when they arrived here and which were torn from them by deliberate government design. The "sophisticates" in north Tel Aviv and Rehavya who look down their noses at the "uncultured" Sephardim must never be allowed to forget that the Jews of the East came here with a deep and abiding culture—Judaism.

Have we already forgotten the Yemenite children, or did we ever want to know about them? When Mapai officials and Mapam camp followers cry out warnings against "fascism," does anyone stop to ask what could have been worse than the actions of the government and the Labor power structure in uprooting the Judaism of the young Jews of Yemen, Morocco, and Iraq? When a certain individual, later a minister in the government, speaks about religious coercion, who reminds him of his role as head of Youth Aliyah in breaking solemn promises to religious parents and sending children with *peyot* (earlocks) to secular centers where the *peyot* and everything they represented disappeared within months?

The political men and women of Labor, who have had a stranglehold on power in the Land of Israel for decades, robbed Jewish children of their Jewish tradition by sending them to irreligious, if not antireligious, institutions and schools. They threatened religious immigrants with loss of jobs and other favors unless they registered their children in irreligious schools. All

The Chosen State: The Jew Within 145

because of their fear that religious children would grow into religious voters and throw Labor out of power. This was excuse enough for snatching their souls from them. Was a more immoral act ever committed by any Right Wing group in the Land? I do not question the fact that the power brokers of Mapai love the state; I only say that they love their party and their power more.

Do we wish to rectify the tragedy of the communal gap, crime, and the erosion of social and moral values? Do we wish to prevent the "Dizengoffization" of Israel? Do we want to return Jews to what the "founding fathers" called values of sacrifice and *halutziut?* And do we, at the same time, wish to fight poverty? The fight cannot be won with money alone. It is not lack of money that is the source of the evil here but the lack of values, the values that were ripped from the Eastern Jews by Mapai and Mapam politicians and never replaced.

I do not totally denigrate the value of *moadanim,* children's recreation centers. But we need only look to the United States for a prime example of the long-range failure of such institutions. The teenager who is lacking in values and an understanding of what is really important in this world will soon grow bored with chess and football and basketball and painting. The streets have a lure for the valueless. All the Mapai brand of ideology and all the Mapam's Borochovian recitations cannot capture them either. What are needed are real values, deep values, *Jewish* values that give them a reason for staying here rather than emigrating to America, Canada, or Australia where there is more money to be made. (And is not material happiness the ultimate desire of man and his rightful goal, as enunciated by both the capitalist and communist thinkers of the world?)

By all means, give the deprived their sports centers and raise money to get them out of the slums. But in the end, if there are no values youth with money in its pocket will become antisocial also. See the Jewish New Left of the West and the growing tragedy of the rootless and confused *bnai tovim,* affluent youth, of Israel. There is hunger in the slums of Israel and it must be relieved. We must give funds for the physical hunger but at least as much energy to the spiritual hunger.

What the politicians of Labor did to the Sephardim was to strip them of the only thing that gave them a feeling of self-respect and self-pride. They could not boast of secular education or wealth, but they came here with the proud knowledge that they and their fathers had cleaved to their Jewish heritage and faith through persecution and degradation. They knew that theirs was the truth and this filled their hearts with the pride of knowing that an immense challenge had been faced and met. When the *kibbutznikim* and the social workers told them that all their tradition was outdated, they were stripped naked. They had nothing left. Except self-contempt and self-hatred.

A person who does not like himself likes no one else. A person who is a self-hater hates the whole world. And let us not underestimate the hatred of the thousands of Sephardim for Askenazim. We delude ourselves because it is pleasanter to do so. We think that the Israeli Black Panthers represent only a tiny, insignificant fringe group.

The Chosen State: The Jew Within **147**

Their numbers are indeed small, but if anyone believes that their thinking does not in large measure mirror the thinking of vast numbers of Eastern Jews, he fools himself. What the Panthers say, many others think. The Panthers have had the audacity to break the silence and they will be followed by many others.

We must do more than give money to the poor of Israel, although that in itself is a matter of the most extreme urgency. We must make the deprived and particularly the Sephardim believe that someone cares—that *we* care. He who is deprived and hopeless is convinced that no one cares about him. If he has an inferiority complex he is convinced of this. Half of the *mitzva* of raising up a brother in need is the simple task of letting him know that someone cares. And we must give the physically and spiritually deprived Sephardic Jew new pride and respect. We must give him a belief in himself, and that can be only done by restoring his values and goals. The government has a clear duty to establish "value centers" in the deprived areas and, I may add, their success will lead the parents of the *bnai tovim* to plead for the same. The greatest obstacle is not money, but the bitter opposition of the Labor power structure. Just as in the case of the revamping of the educational curriculum, here too the Labor people know exactly what is needed for the good of the youth and the state. But they also clearly fear that what is good for the State of Israel is not good for the state of Labor—and Labor takes precedence.

I cannot overemphasize the breakdown in Jewish values and the disaster it has brought to our youth, both affluent and deprived. In this respect the rootlessness, the sense of lack of purpose, the boredom, the search for some meaning to life, is little different among the various classes of Israel. Aside from a large percentage (though not all) of the religious youth, the overwhelming majority of Israeli youth is in a state of limbo, not sure what life is about. There is an intense hunger for material things on the part of those who have not attained wealth and a similar hunger for something else on the part of those who *have* attained it. Both share the feeling that they do not like what they have; both emerge dissatisfied and ever more rebellious and angry.

The less affluent are filled with nonvalues or with sick, western, materialistic ones. There is an abnormal worship of the American golden calf, and everything American is slavishly copied. The hunger for pleasure, for sex, for drugs, for discotheques, for cars, for escape to the affluent West where they can make money, leads to a frustration that erupts into crime, hard violence, sadism, and brutality, a desire to lash out at everyone, and jealousy and hatred of those who possess what they want.

The more affluent have already learned the lesson that man does not live either by bread or by cake, and they search for their own meaning to life. They escape from boredom through drugs and radical politics. They become devotees of the political slogan, the irrational philosophy. They despise their parents, whose life they see as vapid and empty and who cannot give them the answers they want. A culture that is based on materialism, whether covert or overt, is destined to rot away the soul which cannot live within such a world. And so, whether the purpose of life is girls and cars, or study in the university to become a physician and have a nice home, eventually the gnawing boredom and lack of purpose drives man spiritually mad.

This is the lesson of Rome and of the western world today. What has afflicted America and Britain for years is upon us and we have already begun to see its terrible results. But it has only begun. Given a recession or a true crisis, all the materialism and rootlessness could explode into a disastrous upheaval. Those who threw away the discipline and meaningfulness of Jewish values must be prepared to pay in the usual way, by the natural process of eating the fruits of the seeds they themselves have sown.

And is there only a socio-economic communal gap? Is there not also a terrible gap between observant and secular Jew that threatens no less than the other gap, a potential war of brothers? Let us make no mistake about it. The capacity for Jewish fraticide is a historical fact and few doubt that the Arab enemy, while a terrible curse, still has brought us some ironic measure of relief by postponing a potentially tragic clash of Jew against Jew. A war of Jewish brothers was a reality in the past and is a threat for the future. Never was there a more urgent time for Jews to rid themselves of their time-honored, ancient albatross, the inability to act on a problem until the knife is at our throat. The time is now: the time has come to solve our problems before they become insoluble, or soluble only at a terrible cost.

The friction between the religious and the non-religious has reached the danger point. Across a bridgeless chasm the two camps stare at each other with precious little dialogue and conversation. On both sides there are suspicion and mistrust and basic lack of understanding of the other's point of view.

The secularist stares at the religious Jews and sees only that he wishes to circumscribe his freedom to do as he pleases. Because of the religious Jew, he cannot travel on a public conveyance in many cities on the Sabbath; cannot marry the girl of his choice (be she *shiksa* or not); cannot create the kind of free, western society that he reads about in the newspapers. He looks upon the Yeshiva student who is exempt from army service as a draft dodger or an opponent of the state. He moves toward a position where the black kaftan of the Hasid instinctively makes him angry and resentful—without his knowing why. His mind is filled with many false notions and concepts of Judaism: that a Jew, by *halacha,* is only a religious one; that a *mamzer,* bastard, is any child born out of wedlock and thus completely outside of the Jewish community; that the Sabbath and kashrut and ritual purity are meaningless and reasonless relics of medievalism.

The religious Jew stares at the secularist, his way of life, his desecration of Jewish values that to him, the religious Jew, are holy and precious, and considers the secularist to be a maliciously wicked person whose preconceived desire is to destroy Judaism and its practitioners. The whole governmental machinery becomes some sort of diabolical machine whose sole purpose is to crush the Judaism of our fathers. Marxist kibbutzim are peopled with atheistic sinners and the religious Jew must either fight them or have nothing to do with them.

Where there is no dialogue there can be only misunderstanding. When people do not meet each other it is easy for images and demons to take the place of reality. And so is it here.

The secularist who rarely comes into contact with the religious Jew and never sits with him for meaningful discussion of religion, fails to understand that the observant Jew does not live simply to make life difficult and oppressive for a fellow Jew. He has no opportunity to listen to the religious Jew explain that the Jewish people exists only because of and through Torah and that the survival or happiness of the state depend on the observance of the Law. That if we speak of the Defense Forces of Israel, then Jewish history has shown that while Jews do not depend upon miracles and there is a desperate need for Zahal, still, the major defense is observance of *mitzvot* and the study of Torah. And so, with the deepest respect and support for the armed forces, yeshiva students sit and learn—to obtain divine defense for the Jewish state. The secularist rarely has the opportunity to hear the religious Jew say that his very desire to create a truly Jewish state is proof not only of his intense love for Judaism but for all Jews who live in the state. It would be easy enough not to care about how the secularist lives; it is a sign of love that one cares enough about a fellow Jew to try to make him cleave to his heritage despite his lack of understanding of its importance.

To be sure there are the few, the religious minority, whose bitterness against the desecration of Torah has driven them to a point of unreasoning hatred of the secularist. But the secularist does not understand that this kind of mind just as easily, perhaps more easily, hates the observant Jew who is not quite as ready to hate the secular Jew. The kind of Jew who refuses to recognize the state, hates and despises the observant Zionist Jew even more than he hates the atheist Marxist one. Nor does the secularist understand what a minority of a minority this group is within religious Jewry and how unacceptable is its point of view to religious Jews. And so he makes the grave error of equating all religious Jews with a few at the very monent that he deplores the blaming of all *kibbutznikim* for the sins of *their* few. This error can only be erased by the secularist's being willing to sit down with the religious Jew and hear his side of the argument— a side, incidentally, which was the mainstream of Judaism for millennia.

Only this dialogue will allow the secularist to understand the contention that the *halacha*—which has been the very air of the Jew since Sinai—has at least the same right to limit the individual that socialism has. That the very essence of a state is its right to limit the individual's freedom in return for what it promises him will be a greater good. That many individuals are unconvinced of this greater good and thus lament the loss of their freedom, but so long as the democratic majority decrees that it sees the logic of the "trade," this remains the rule of the land and cannot be attacked as "coercive" or "oppressive." All laws of society are coercive in the sense that they force the individual to obey even when he does not particularly care to. All the state's laws are oppressive in the sense that they take from me the delicious freedom to do anything I would like to do. But any sensible man knows that they are not oppressive in the pejorative sense of the word. The price we pay for making man safer and better is individual liberty.

If Socialism can take away man's right to work as hard as he can, keep all that he makes, and let the poor devil hang who was not as clever or as fortunate, none of the "progressives" calls this coercive or oppressive. If religion, in order to make man a more disciplined and less selfish person, and in order to obtain what it believes to be G-d's divine intervention on behalf of the state, does the same thing, why should it be considered tyrannical?

Dialogue is what we need and Ahavat Yisroel and a willingness to hear the other side. And this goes for the religious Jew, too.

How difficult it is for one who believes to understand the mind of one who does not. How difficult to place one's self in the shoes of a man whose training, whose education, whose environment are so different. Is a *kibbutznik* of Hashomer Hatzair to be condemned because he never saw a pair of *tefillin* or a Torah scroll in his life until he joined the army? Is one who was subject to totally secular, or even atheist and Marxist indoctrination, wicked? How simplistic and how terribly un-Jewish to hold such views. Only the man who secretly wishes the majority to remain secular so that he may be numbered among the few, the "elite," will not look upon the secularist as one who simply either did not receive a full, effective Jewish education or as one who, for whatever reason, left the observance of the faith. Not hatred and not pushing aside and not separate communities will solve the religious-irreligious confict, but an understanding of each side, a mature willingness to recognize that there can be honest differences (even when each side is convinced that it is correct), that these differences need not stem from wicked intention, that compromises are necessary for the people and state to survive.

What do I mean by compromises? Not on questions of principle; Not that the religious should agree to change a *halacha* for the sake of a nebulous peace. But that each side, when pushing for a change in the status quo, should realize just what is noncompromisable and what had better be left alone. For the irreligious it is imperative to realize that on certain issues that affect the very heart and root of the Jewish definition there can be no compromise by religious Jews. No rabbi can be asked to twist or bend *halacha*—no matter how important it may seem to the secularist. The religious understands that although Torah never changes, the times and tempers of the times do change and what a society was willing to accept once, it may not be willing to accept now. That, in the end, it is impossible to force upon an unwilling majority that which it will not agree to. That certain areas, although of great importance, do not go to the heart of the definition of the Jew and if not pushed today can still be pushed at a later date when times and tempers change. That to push and win a battle at the wrong time is sometimes to lose the war later on.

How sad that so many of the leaders of both camps are men who add little honor to their cause. Let us not judge the cause by the incompetence or pettiness of certain of its representatives. The main thing is for the Jews of the state who love their nation and land to understand that they cannot separate themselves from their Jewishness that brought them back and that some means must be found and can be found to live together. Bridges, dialogue, and Ahavat Yisroel are the burning needs of the hour.

I do not say that the parties to dialogue will walk away from their conversation agreeing to agree. But when one sits down with another for a discussion of deep differences and leaves agreeing to disagree, a major success has been achieved. For the two have heard each other, understand that there is honesty and sincerity on both sides, and begin to see *why* the other side differs. Dialogue should leave the one who truly believes unshaken in his convictions, but with new compassion and insight for his opponents. In the end every Jew is a Jew no more or less than others. Good or bad, he is our brother and we love him.

7

The Chosen State: Character and Personality

If the Jewish state is the receptacle of the Jewish people, exists to serve it and to ingather it, is created to reflect Judaism and Jewishness in practice, then it must surely have a character and personality that is unmistakenly Jewish and leaves no room for doubt on that subject.

It is not just a question of "religion," and it is not only for the "religious" Jew to consider it as something vital and nonnegotiable. The very fabric and definition of the nation are involved, and every Jewish nationalist

The Chosen State: Character and Personality 157

must be concerned to see that the national identity not be contaminated by assimilation. If there are those who so correctly worry over the ruination of inanimate national treasures, such as forest, green spaces, and beaches, how much more should we be concerned over the ideological pollution of our national character.

The Jewish state must reflect the Jewish people and we must never lose sight of the definition of that people. To speak of a Jewish religion as something distinct from a Jewish nation or to speak of the possibility of the absence of either concept is to misunderstand, to pervert, and to deny the Jewish truth of the Jewish people.

The Jewish people exists as a religio-nation and to be considered a Jew is to partake of both qualities. The single Jew is but a reflection of his whole people and *he* is what *it* is. The rules of the Jewish "game" have been set and although there may be those who do not like it, that is irrelevant. If the rules are changed the game is no longer the same. The Jewish people is not subject to the whims of the transitory majority, let alone of the relative few. A nation that has survived only because of its iron discipline to its definition of self cannot and will not change its historical truth at the behest of even an entire generation, which comes and goes within the twinkling of a historical eye.

Thus the eternal fusion of religion and nation is what makes the specific uniqueness of the Jew, and one must not only reject but fight to the bitter end those who would impose the sanction of legal change on this definition. No body, no matter how prestigious or respected, can change the definition of a Jew. None can, by fiat, bestow the title "Jew" upon a Christian, and none can separate nation from faith. None can define a Jew in any other way than the traditional, historical, religio-national way. And the Jewish state, as a mere servant and receptacle of the Jewish people, can do no more and no less. A Jew, in the eyes of the Jewish state, can be only that person who fits the historical and eternal definition: one is a Jew both in nationality and religion.

One does not become a Jew or leave off becoming a Jew through some personal whim. Jewishness is not a game that one can stop playing when boredom or disillusion set in. It is not a game that one plays by his own rules and where decisions, such as when to start and when to stop, are made by the individual player. Judaism is not a reward for being good and cannot be bestowed because of the good character of the individual, just as it cannot be taken away merely because of his obnoxious behavior to his people.

A Jew is one who is born of a Jewish mother—this is the view of *halacha* that has been accepted from the days of Sinai until very recently. He can be a bad Jew in that he is a traitor to his people, turns his back on them, or even actively works against them. Let us curse such a man, let us work to stop his evil designs, let us even go further—but there is one thing that we cannot do. We cannot cast him out of the Jewish camp. We must suffer his presence like any family striken by the presence within its midst of a son who has shamed and defiled it. By his actions he does not cease to be their son.

The Chosen State: Character and Personality 159

A Jew is also one who, having been born a gentile, chooses honestly, deeply, and sincerely to become a practicing and faithful Jew. But here there is a difference. The son who was *born* to us is ours and we have no choice but to accept him and keep him regardless of his conduct. The stranger who comes out of the night and *asks* to become part of the family undergoes far greater and deeper inspection. His is not a right but a privilege, and he must pay for that privilege by adhering to the demands and conditions that we set for him. And the most basic of these is to be a practicing Jew who will add honor and respect to the family he claims to love and admire.

Hardly an unreasonable demand. The Jewish people —particularly in this age of unfaithful sons and daughters —is hardly in great need of more unfaithfulness. The Jewish nation is not a people that hungers after numbers: "For you are the least among the nations." It is not quantity that is the dream of Judaism but quality, and he who seeks entry into the unique and chosen people is asked to partake of that uniqueness by his actions. No one sought him out, no one pleaded with him to come into the Jewish tent; ours is not the hungry way of the missionary. We welcome all into the goodly tents of Jacob, but the conditions are stiff and only the worthy may comply and join.

It is acceptance of *halacha,* Jewish practice, that marks the distinctiveness of the Jew. This is the principle demand; this is how one is recognized as a Jew; this is what makes the Jew different from the man he was before. Not merely social justice, for while this is truly a worthy and noble ideal—indeed, the essence of man's life—it is not specifically Jewish. One who comes and says: "I desire to change my life and my people," does not merely go through some meaningless ritual and then continue in the same non-unique path as before, no matter how noble that path is. He makes a change. And that change comprises both the social justice that has been accepted by the gentiles and also the distinctiveness of the Jewish *mitzva* between man and G-d. The acceptance of *halacha* is the proof of the sincerity of the conversion.

The very hesitation of the gentile to do this is already a clear mark that he is not prepared to bow to the yoke of Jewishness. His refusal to accept the *manner* of conversion reflects his future refusal to accept other aspects of Jewishness. The new Jew is expected to worship the *Jewish* G-d, not his own wishes and ideology or even his personal *view* of that Jewish G-d.

Since time immemorial, *halacha* has declared just who is a Jew and how one becomes a Jew. Indeed, there are cases, few and far between, wherein good and noble people who have sacrificed much for the Jewish people under the illusion that they were Jewish, have been told that *halacha* decrees otherwise. Is this a tragedy? Only for the one who refuses to take the simple steps that will bring him legally into the people he claims to love so much. Is the good "Jew" who refuses on principle to undergo *halachic* conversion a tragic figure? Hardly. He is a stubborn figure and that is his right, but Judaism survived all these years because it

The Chosen State: Character and Personality 161

was more stubborn than those who would have destroyed it or changed it. It dare not bow to the will of any human being lest it lose all pretense of being divine.

Those in the Galut who perform conversions contrary to *halacha* are invariably of the school that twisted Jewishness beyond recognition, that fought the concept of maximum Jewish nationalism, that perverted religion into a meaningless cant of convenience. It is hardly for them to complain about the refusal of the Jewish state to sanction their perversions. That which they polluted in the Galut, let them not bring here. There is no epic tragedy when *halachic* conversion is refused. Every nation has its rules. The alien who seeks to come into the state may not be happy with the conditions of entry but he has his choice: Accept them or do not enter. No one forces him to do either. His is the choice when he refuses to accept either the logic or rationale of the dictating state. There may be individual "principle" involved here, there may be political issues, and there may be personal ego and stubbornness, but let us not speak of epic tragedy. A man may dwell for decades in a state and assume that this should morally bestow citizenship upon him, but it does not. He must still do what all others do and apply through the legal channels. If he refuses he has no right to complain. The door to citizenship and equal status with others is before him. He needs only to move his feet. If he refuses to, for whatever reason, let him stop complaining about compulsion.

I have deliberately not spoken yet about the question of splitting the nation but surely this is something that truly dedicated Jews will consider to be the most important of considerations. The Jew who believes that the origin of the Jewish people began at Sinai with the creation of a religio-nation, with the nation committed to a specific Jewish teaching and way of life, is the Jew who considers *halacha* as that way of life. We are not dealing here with a political or economic ideology that is subject to basic compromise and good will. To be sure, good will is needed within the broadest possible framework of *halacha*. But good will cannot make of it what it is not. It cannot create something from nothing or nothing from something.

Halacha is a way of life and any rabbi and Jewish judge who is not blessed with the warmth and compassion to stretch *halacha* to its outermost limits in order to find leniency betrays his task. *Koach d'heteyra adif* (the power of leniency takes priority) is surely one of the great maxims of Jewish law, and the efforts of the great Jewish rabbinic leaders in history to find *koach d'heteyra,* leniency, are legendary. How much effort and how much struggle must be put into the most learned of attempts to find a solution of leniency. But leniency must be based on truth and must be culled from *halacha* itself. If *halacha* is to have any meaning it cannot become a figurehead, a mere ornament. *Halacha* lives and guides us and while we shine the light of leniency upon it, we cannot see in it that which is not there or ignore that which is patently apparent.

We have been subject in recent years to ignorant, unlearned statements concerning the "House of Hillel" and "Shammai." Ignoramuses who do not believe in *halacha* at all have dinned into our ears the thought that those who do not desire to bend—and break—*halacha* to suit them are tyrants of the House of Shammai, the traditionally stricter Talmudic school. The charges reflect only on the empty heads of those who level them. Neither the House of Hillel nor the House of Shammai of Talmudic times sought to purposely ban or allow. *Halacha* was a thing that was true whatever the ruling was, strict or lenient, and none sought to curry favor with politicians or others.

Both schools sought to rule with truth. Each school sought to find leniency when it thought it was possible. Each loved Jews deeply and their lives were spent seeking happiness for all Jews.

Thus, there are many things that the power of leniency can create and avert but there are some things that are clear and unbending for none to deny. Certain things compel us to say: *"Hadin yikov et ha'har"* ("Let the law pierce the mountain.") The definition of a Jew is fixed by *halacha,* it is not subject to the whims and vagaries and false leniencies of the transitory times. And if *halacha* speaks out clearly and finally, the Jew who is bound by *halacha* and who understands that but for it there is no reason for separate Jewish existence—let alone a state of its own—cannot and will not budge from its truth.

The Knesset may vote overwhelmingly to define a Jew in any way it sees fit, but the *halachic* Jew will stand and say: You have no right, you have no power, your definition is not binding. And it will not be.

Thus it will happen that the *halachic* Jew will refuse to recognize the Knesset-created Jew as a Jew. And let us understand something whose understanding is long overdue.

The *halachic* Jew is not only the chasid of Mea Shearim. He is not only the Jew of the kaftan and the earlocks. He is also the Jew who serves and falls with the defense forces, the Jew of the religious kibbutz movement, the hundreds of thousands of Jews of Israel who believe in the divinity of Torah and the sancrosanctity of *halacha.* He is the Jew of misnamed and misunderstood Beit Hillel and Beit Shammai. In a word, there is not an observant Jew in the state who will recognize a definition of a Jew that is not based on *halacha.* Here, the Jews of *Kibbutz Ha'dati* will join hands with the men of Mea Shearim. The result will be a disastrous and irrevocable split of the Jewish people. Worse, it will be a needless split, and it is time for the defenders of *halacha* to cease their defensive posture and cry out that it will be a split brought about because of the stubbornness, intransigence, and irrational hatred of religion on the part of the opponents of *halacha.*

For the *halachic* Jew there is a religious principle here that outweighs life itself. For his opponents there is neither principle nor argument. There is no argument, for the one who truly wishes to become Jewish is not barred but only told to follow the *halachic* procedures. And there is no principle, for the real reason for the vociferous obstinacy of the extreme opponents of *halacha* is their deep-seated hatred of the religious. It is not any one area of religion that they fight. Their real aim is the uprooting of religion as a meaningful force in Jewish life. If we speak of extremists in Israel, mention of the secular extremist circles is long overdue.

There is no need for a split. There is only the need

to recognize how much this definition of a Jew means to the *halachic* Jew, how much, to him, this goes to the very core of Jewish existence. It calls for the most elementary respect for the deepest feelings of a fellow Jew as measured against the far shallower opposition to those feelings. It calls for the knowledge that the individual who truly wishes to become a Jew is not barred from doing so except by his own stubbornness. Above all, it calls for deep introspection and self-criticism, the questioning of oneself: Is it really so important to me that I should split the Jewish nation in half? Those who so easily castigate the observant Jew for his alleged lack of *Ahavat Yisroel* would do well to ask themselves whether there is any greater danger to that concept than their own conduct in opposing the *halachic* definition of a Jew. The time has come to isolate the psychopathic leftists and pseudo-intellectuals whose hatred of religion so effectively mirrors their own self-disgust.

There is a similarly needless and disastrous clash on the question of civil marriage. *Halacha* certainly offers the way of leniency in all but the fewest of cases. There is no doubt that certain marriages are forbidden, such as Jew to non-Jew, incestuous unions, *kohen* (priest) to divorcee, *mamzer* (bastard) (only one who is the offspring of an incestuous or adulterous relationship) to non-*mamzer*. We shall not play games. These are forbidden marriages and no rabbi will perform them.

And so there is a cry: Civil marriage! Or a more elegant one: Civil marriage for those who are barred from religious marriage. I shall add only a word or two here about those whose real aim is not civil marriage but also civil divorce, something that would increase the number of *mamzerim* disastrously. Civil marriage is but a first step leading to civil divorce, which will truly split the nation into two camps, with one refusing to marry into the other. If this is what we truly want it is ours for the asking.

But for those who are sincerely troubled by the refusal on the part of the rabbinate to marry certain couples, let us examine those disabled couples.

It is true that under no circumstances whatever does *halacha* recognize an incestuous marriage, and there may indeed be some who will insist that a civil law should be created to allow marriage between mother and son or brother and sister on the grounds that the law should not limit any conduct so long as that conduct does not harm others. It may be true that there will be those who will—as in certain western countries—insist on recognizing the marriage of two homosexual males or females. For these, *halacha* has no answer; its ban is clear and absolute and one hopes that the proponents of civil marriage in these cases will be accorded the contempt they deserve.

Then there is the question of intermarriage. True, there is absolutely no sanction, a priori or a posteriori, for intermarriage under *halacha*. A Jew is forbidden to marry a non-Jew; his marriage will not be performed by a rabbi; it will not be recognized under any circumstances. There are, indeed, more than a few among the nihilists in our ranks who oppose this. They would open the doors to the disaster that Jews fought so successfully through two millennia of Exile and to which they succumb so disastrously in the "free" western world. The destruction of the Jew can be accomplished in the furnaces of Auschwitz; it can also come about through intermarriage that destroys the Jewish identity of the couple and its offspring. One hopes that the vast majority of nationalistic Jews will understand the vital importance, to the existence of the Jewish nation, of the *halachic* ban on intermarriage, and will reject the demands of those who, had they been the Jews of the Middle Ages, would have guaranteed that today a problem such as this one would not exist, since they would long since have assimilated out of existence.

But there are other bans. Consider the ban on marriage between *kohen* and divorcee or *mamzer* and non-*mamzer* or a number of other bans mentioned in the Torah. The rabbinate will refuse to marry these. Is it then not "fair" to allow them to utilize civil marriage? Before replying, let us understand something that is basic to Judaism.

What is "fair" or not "fair" within the context of human understanding is not always the simple thing it is made out to be by simplistic people. What is "right" and what is "not right" for the Jew has never been a subjective thing, to be judged by man on the basis of his own cultural imperative. It has certainly never been something to be measured by transient, temporary standards. That which has been true for generations cannot be dislodged with nary a thought because of the impatience of one generation, though it be the latest in the chain of history. The Jews are an eternal people with eternal values, and eternity is not subject to the passing modes and fashions of ideology. The Jews are a divine people with divine values, and these infinite truths are not to be passed upon or rejected by finite and human animals.

Halacha has been the savior of the Jewish people, that which allowed it to survive through the impossibility of Exile; that which gave it strength, pride, and self-respect; that which gave meaning to existence, an existence that is so meaningless and subject to so much doubt for those who rejected *halacha*. The greatness and sole strength of *halacha* lies in its divinity, otherwise why cling to it? And that strength is decimated and the pillar upon which it stands is eliminated when it must give way before a generation that cries "Unfair." Unfair to finite eyes, perhaps, but the individual whom this "unfairness" touches must bow to the majesty and greatness of a *halacha* which alone saved a people, gave it strength to continue, and bestows upon it the majesty of eternity. What law is "fair" to all people and what society does not demand a few sacrifice so that society may continue to exist? And one day, the one who was touched by "unfairness" will understand that it was not really so. It is not by the standards of finite "fairness" that the Jewish people and *halacha* abide. Let the law pierce the mountain, but the law must prevail. Or we, as a people, will not prevail.

But there is more. Those who cry for civil marriage say that this is the only solution. Is that really true? Is it a solution? And if that solution is considered a solution, then is there not a far better way, one that does not question the absolute supremacy and authority of *halacha*?

The Chosen State: Character and Personality 169

What will happen if a civil marriage law is passed in Israel? Will the rabbinate recognize it? Will the religious community recognize it? The answer is negative in both cases. But that does not matter, is the retort. We are not interested in whether the rabbinate or the religious Jew recognizes it. We want it to be recognized officially by the state.

So, this is what apparently really troubles the proponents of civil marriage. That under present law the state will not marry one non-*halachically.* Is this the problem? For this there is no need for civil marriage; to solve this problem there is no need at all to introduce the non-Jewish concept of civil marriage, a thing that threatens to be only the first step toward civil divorce that would catastrophically divide the nation.

Halacha itself gives a way out. For while, a priori, no rabbi will perform a marriage banned by *halacha,* all marriages that are forbidden marriages—except those involving gentiles and incest—are recognized as marriages by the Torah a posteriori even though the couples disobeyed the injunction against them.

Let us consider the case of a *kohen* and a divorcee or a *mamzer* and non-*mamzer.* Faced with the refusal of a rabbi to marry them what would happen if, in the presence of two proper witnesses, the man betrothed the woman unto him? Such a marriage is a binding one, calling for a divorce to dissolve it, and although the two have sinned and disobeyed the Torah, the marriage is valid. Certainly the religious stigma remains, but would that stigma be any less under civil marriage? And, in any case, do the opponents of *halacha* really care? Assuming that they are sincere in their avowals that their sole purpose is to allow the couple to be married and have their marriage recognized by the state, there is no need to introduce civil marriage. The state can insist that the marriage be recorded as a legal one, reading "married—in a priori violation of Torah law." The additional wording should in no way bother those who are not interested in Torah law and who have achieved all that they say they wanted—a recognized state marriage.

To say that there are no problems that *halacha* cannot solve to the satisfaction of the secular public would be to lie. But *halacha,* unlike politicians, did not come into being to cater to the public but rather to raise it, uplift it, and sanctify it. On the other hand, the numbers of cases that pose permanent problems are very few in number, and it is only the voices of the demagogues who magnify the problem for their own ends.

This chapter is titled "The Chosen State—Character and Personality." I repeat that the Jewish people has a peculiar, distinct, separate, and holy character and that the state must both recognize this and incorporate that distinctiveness and holiness into itself. The state and the society within it must be clearly recognized as a Jewish state and society. From the *mezuzot* that should be affixed to the public gates—even in predominantly non-Jewish areas—to the laws dealing with the identity of the Jewish people and their personal status, to the public scene, everything should cry out the the beholder: You see, this is the Jewish state!

The religio-national character of the Jewish people must find voice and substance in the state that it calls its own. The offensive behavior of a national Jewish organization in the Galut that schedules a nonkosher dinner as part of its "Jewish" activities or that publicly desecrates the Jewish Sabbath, is no more offensive than the Jewish state that desecrates its national character through state violations of *halacha*. It does not matter that the individual is nonobservant. When he represents a Jewish group he represents Jewish tradition and honor. And the state, although it be made up of a majority of secular people, in its capacity as a state represents Jewishness and Judaism. How utterly lacking in any semblance of self-respect for the Jewish state to spit in the face of its own Jewish tradition that is responsible for its existence in the first place.

In the end we must blend together our respect for tradition and the character of our people and state with tolerance and good will. Such is the way of peace and Jewish existence. Any other path is that of deadly hate, civil strife, and Jewish disaster. At the same time, however, let us never forget that we came here to the Land of Israel to build a Jewish, not a western country. It is Jewish values that are true, not western values (or eastern, for that matter). What is right and true is not to be determined by liberalism or democracy or progressive circles. Our youth must be imbued with *Jewish* concepts and our state must be shaped and characterized by them.

8
The Destiny

And so it is time to sum up. What is written here is an idea. It is not a new idea. It is the ancient, majestic, eternally glorious idea of Judaism, the idea that was the mainstream of Jewish thinking throughout history and that within recent times became lost, modified, and confused. It is a call to return to that idea, to the only Judaism and Jewishness that makes any kind of logical sense and serves any sort of logical reason for continuity. It is a call to change a land of Jews into a Jewish land. Above all, it is a call for greatness.

The Jewish people and state are not just one more people and state—they are spiritually greater than all the rest. We are not simply one more little, superfluous nation but the heart and the reason for the world. We will not be allowed to be small and indifferent, but rather a people of greatness, of sacrifice, of majesty. We dare not opt for mediocrity, smallness of vision, or the ordinary. We have been chosen for a great role, one that demands of us the ability to reject superficiality, to understand what is important and what is vain nonsense, and to be prepared to sacrifice in order to reach the spiritual heights. Israel will never be one more nation like all the nations. It will be a special and unique place to build the Jewish society.

Perhaps the greatest sin of those who lead the state is their refusal or inability to recognize the miracle and uniqueness of the Jewish people and state. They have treated the great events of our time with mundaneness, as part of a magnificent but normal course of history. They have treated Jews like any other people, albeit more clever or tenacious, and the state as arising from blood and valor, but basically the same as any other state. They refuse to recognize the divine quality and uniqueness of the Jew and his state and are embarrassed and angry when these special qualities and destiny are spoken about. That which the Almighty has given us time after time in our days has been downgraded, profaned, and made normal and secular by the leaders of the state. In a sense, it must be sadly stated, they have cheapened the people, and their punishment is that the people have come to accept the secularization of the miracle of Return.

All that must be changed. We must recognize our greatness, we must acknowledge our uniqueness, we must greet the miracle of our times with the awe and joy that they deserve. We must look at ourselves in the mirror of history and gasp: "We are indeed a spiritually great and unique people and we live in an era of divine redemption! Our land must be a *Jewish* one, with the idea expressed in a state whose character and thinking are Jewish." We must learn to allow the love of each and every Jew to fill our minds and hearts and never to permit ourselves to narrow our identity to any one community. There is no American Jew, there is no Yemenite Jew, there is no Israeli Jew. There remains only *the* Jew. For us, Jewish problems come first. For us, there is no illusion of permanent allies *except* the Jew. For us, there can be no dichotomy, no split loyalties: all our loyalty is to one "ism," Judaism. For us, the yardstick by which we judge a problem, our actions and reactions, remains: Is it good for the Jew?

Much that I say here will bring down the wrath of the assimilated Jew, yet I insist once again that such a Jew exists by the hundreds of thousands within the Jewish state. His is the assimilation of ideas, his is the absorption of foreign bodies and concepts so that he no longer recognizes what is Jewish thinking. He will cry out and protest and condemn. He may be joined by others who are afraid to think the unthinkable and speak the unspeakable even though it may be true.

If there is one thing that a Jew must always

The Destiny 175

remember it is that although the vast majority says "No," if he, the Jew, believes "Yes," he will continue to believe, to teach, and to do. We are the sons of Abraham Ha'Ivri, the one from the other side. And our rabbis teach us that it was the one man Abraham who stood on the one side of a belief while the whole world stood on the other, and who dared to say: "I am right."

Noisy journalists and loud politicians are not always right and neither is the majority, necessarily. The Jew has always been a minority and has always had the courage and the "brazenness" to insist that his is the right way. What do the people say? Do they agree? That is not the point. If you believe that you are right, say it. In time, they will understand and accept it. Yours is not to fear unacceptability or unpopularity but rather to serve as a gadfly, as the one who knows what must be said and what must be done, and who says and does it first, the one who gives the timid courage to follow. That which the man of courage says today, the timid majority will proclaim tomorrow; that which the lonely minority dares to do now, the myopic will later understand and copy. The man of vision has a task—to drag the unwilling up the path of greatness. And although they stone him today, tomorrow they will pay him the greatest of all flattery, imitation.

There are many Jews within the Land who agree with what has been written here. There are many who know that a change must take place and that the reins of government should be given over to those with maximum Jewish values. There are many who realize that much good has been done by those who have been in power all these years but that the things that have not been done or that have been undone are far more dangerous, although they may not be seen as yet, and that we live in an illusion that will be dispelled only when it is very late.

But even these Jews are stricken by that national malady, hopelessness. There is a sense of cynical despair and a feeling that nothing can be changed. The same people, the same group, the same leaders have been in power all these years and no one has ever been able to move them out. The legendary power of the government becomes a smothering blanket that paralyzes any real will to change.

The Rebbe of Kotzk once pondered over the *halacha psuka* (clear law) that one who finds a lost item in the street need not return it, although he knows who the owner is and where he lives, so long as he also knows that the loser of the object has despaired of finding it.

"How is it possible," asked the Hasidic sage, "that the holy and righteous Torah should not make it incumbnent upon a finder who knews the loser's identity to return the item to him?"

"But," replied the Kotzker, "there is a punishment here, a fine upon the loser of the object. He lost hope. He despaired. A Jew is not allowed to lose hope!"

Things can be changed because they *must* be changed. Only the hopeless will drink the bitter dregs of their own hopelessness, and they will deserve to. Others will know that change occurs when there is a total, dedicated ideology and effort, a determination to move on to Jewish destiny and to teach and put into effect the eternal Jewish truths.

We must instill in our youth, and in ourselves, deep national pride, but we must realize, too, that all the secular nationalism in the world will not suffice to justify Jewish exclusiveness. It is only religion that justifies nationalism and, indeed, it is impossible to speak of Judaism without connecting the two. Judaism is religio-nationalism.

And if it is true that there can be no Judaism if the religious aspect of nationalism is removed, it follows that there can be no meaningful Judaism if the national aspect of religion is removed. Perhaps the greatest error and sin of the religious camp is in its acquiescence in the narrowing of the religious concept. Among the secular Jews, one does not equate great Jewish problems with the religious leadership. There have arisen in the minds of the public "national" problems and "religious" ones. Ask the secularist what the religious parties and leaders are interested in and he will immediately think of Shabbat or kashrut or marriage and divorce. He will never connect religious circles with the leadership in the struggle for "national" questions. It is not they who, in his mind, are in the forefront in the battle for Soviet or Syrian Jewry, the struggle to retain the liberated lands, or the fight against Arab terror. And the absence of religious leadership here, their acquiescence in the separation of religious issues from "national" ones is a falsification of Judaism. The religious sectors have, in practice, narrowed the meaning of religion and thus have crippled Judaism.

To be religious *is* to be nationalist. Shabbat is no less but no more of interest and concern to the observant Jew than the territories and security and Soviet and

Syrian Jewry. We must return to the original definition of Judaism as a religio-national concept, a concern for *all* aspects of Jewish life. Just as the Sabbath or marriage and divorce are not "religious" problems but Jewish religio-national ones, so are the so-called "secular" or "national" problems Jewish religio-national ones.

The limiting and narrowing of Judaism must change as must the inferiority complex that has seized so many religio-national Jews. They have come to believe the libel spread by the professional anti-religious, that they are somehow less nationalistic or patriotic than the secularist. Enough of that. The time has come for self-pride and the sure knowledge that the religio-national way is the Jewish way. The time has come to create a proud and dynamic religio-national camp that not only reacts, but acts, that takes the lead on all issues in Jewish life, that evokes respect and admiration. The time has come to express firmly and loudly the religio-national truths:

The Jewish nation, formed at Sinai as a divine religio-nation; chosen, special, hallowed, and set apart with an eternal mission to study, practice, and model themselves by the Torah.

A nation that is bound by eternal and unbreakable bonds; whose every Jew is brother and sister to every other Jew; whose obligation of Ahavat Yisroel demands the utmost love and sacrifice on behalf of a suffering Jew; whose unity is clear and is not divided by false and artificial boundaries of class struggle; and whose Jewish interests take precedence over those of others.

A land that is hallowed and given to us by the

Creator and Possessor of all the earth; which is not given over to partition; which is not the property or right of any other people.

A state which is the trustee of all the Jewish people, which has the right to demand support from them and which has, in return, the obligation to protect them; which must work to bring them home from the four corners of the earth.

A state that must teach its own citizens the meaning of Ahavat Yisroel so as to overcome the evils of poverty, social injustice, and anarchy of values; that must learn to bridge the chasm of hate between differing groups.

A state that must teach its youth that they are part of the Jewish people *before* they are part of the Israeli state or of themselves: that must teach its youth the beauties of its heritage and Judaism from childhood on.

A state that must be *Jewish*—not western or secular or like the other nations—in its character and personality and behavior.

A people, land, and state with a destiny that is sure and unchangeable.

We live, today, in the dawn of the final redemption, and the footsteps of the Messiah can be clearly heard. The Jewish Destiny is determined and no force on earth can prevent its coming. The question remains whether we will hasten it so that it comes swiftly and painlessly or whether its arrival will be delayed and arrive only after needless suffering and tragedy. "I am the L-rd, in its time will I hurry it (the redemption)." These words of the Prophet Isaiah are brought down by the rabbis of the Talmud who ask: "If the redemption comes in 'its time' then how will G-d 'hurry it?' And if He hurries it, then it will not arrive in 'its time?'" And they reply: "If Israel merits the redemption by repentance and faith in the Jewish G-d, then He will hurry the redemption before its time. *But even if Israel does not merit it, it will surely come in its appointed time."*

There is an appointed time for the Jewish Destiny to reach fulfillment, and no power or superpower in the world can stand in the way of the Divine decree. The tragedy, however, remains the Jewish refusal to merit it and thus hasten the Redemption so that it arrives swiftly, with breathtaking glory and with a minimum of tragedy and suffering. It is within our power to demand from the Almighty that He deliver the Jewish people and establish His Kingdom. All we need do is return to the law and to faith in Him. But even if we do not, though we will pay heavily for it in terms of lives and pain, let us never forget that there is "an appointed time," *and that time is now.* He who does not believe this, though his eyes have seen the magnificent miracles of our days, is truly blind. The State of Israel, as the people who give it its name, is indestructible. Let us stop wailing over the irrelevant and meaningless threats from empty and transitory superpowers. If we believe and we return to G-d, if we believe and refuse to compromise the great miracle of our time by withdrawal and retreat, the Redemption is within our hands. Fear, confusion, hopelessness? Quite the opposite!

What will be the end? The Messiah will come and bring all our people home, there to create a state that will be a light unto the nations. Until then, it is our task to survive, to reach out to our Jewishness and to live up to our unique, chosen, and separate role: the creation of a Torah people and state. Indeed, there is a need for a *spiritual* Jewish Defense League, one that will call for policies designed to defend Jews spiritually as well as physically.

Let us not be ashamed of that role and of our task. Let us not be driven from it by the sneers and the smears of the ignorant and the self-haters. Let us, by all means, love each and every one of them, but let us insist that they face the central question: Will Israel be a *Jewish* state or not?

Shame? Quite the opposite. Rather pride, satisfaction, and joy in the challenge.

"Happy are we, how good is our portion, and how pleasant our lot, and how beautiful our inheritance."